MUMs
RECIPES
THREE

Produced for
Malawi Underprivileged Mothers

by
Linda McDonald RGN, RM

Published by **Linda McDonald**
www.mumsrecipes.org

Printed October 2009
ISBN no: 0-9551690-3-8
Registered Charity no: SC037759

Illustrations drawn by **Sally McDonald**

Designed & printed by **Smart Design & Print Ltd**
www.smartdesignandprint.com

CONTENTS

FOREWORD by Sarah Brown

I first met Linda McDonald at my bedside as I held my first newborn son who had arrived safely in the New Royal Infirmary Edinburgh. After the loss of my first baby, my daughter Jennifer, just under two years earlier, I felt I understood everything about the most painful grief imaginable. Linda was one of the midwives who guided me through the first nights with my wonderful little son and I know just how good she is. We chatted a lot during the early hours while John slept and I heard all about her passion for the people of Malawi, her determination to help in a practical way to bring pregnant mums and newborns a better chance of life by providing quality skilled professional healthcare. For all my heartbreak, what I know is that I received the best of healthcare. Everything possible was done for me and my family with the privilege of the National Health Service available to us.

The first two 'MUMs Recipes' books have raised vital funds to contribute to the new Bwaila Hospital and to support a programme for the prevention of mother to child HIV/AIDS transmission plus a new Wellness Centre in Lilongwe in Malawi. I was so proud to play a small part contributing the foreword in the second volume and couldn't be more delighted that Linda has invited me to say a few words again.

Since 2003, when I met Linda, I have gone on to have a second son (again with Linda by my side in the nighttime – and that time hearing even more about her determined engagement with the Malawi nurses and health workers to encourage them to stay and work locally). I too have followed my own commitment to improving maternal and newborn health, engaging with an international campaign to reduce the number of deaths during pregnancy and childbirth. Today – in the 21st Century - it is still the case that over 500,000 mums die giving birth just at the time when they should be happiest, and newborns are 10 times more likely to die if they lose their mum. At the international level things are starting to change – Presidents and Prime Ministers are stepping up to the plate to make the changes needed to bring in more professional health workers, more health centres and more vital equipment and supplies properly distributed.

This is what Linda understands, and more than that, she knows that it takes each community, each hospital, each group of citizens to take on the challenge. Linda's project is centred in Malawi, where she and her husband, Iain, have recently returned from a six month stay doing what they love – rolling up their sleeves and making a difference. They have been helping create better facilities for the women of Lilongwe – and are saving lives every day. And more than that back in Scotland, Linda's work helps all of us understand better just what it takes to make that difference – and how all of us can contribute to that by buying this book. It is no wonder that Edinburgh made Linda their Citizen of the Year in 2008 – a proud moment and a great acknowledgement of her contribution.

Earlier this year, TV presenter and Comic Relief regular, Davina McCall, agreed to make a film about maternal mortality for the 2009 Red Nose Day in Malawi. She travelled out there with the BBC camera team and knew that this would be an important and challenging trip. I asked her to look out for Linda and was delighted to get a text to say they had met up. Davina's film is one of the most moving pieces ever made for Comic Relief (and that is saying something) and this was reflected in the level of generosity of the British public, who responded overwhelmingly. I know that Linda helped to bring home the reality of giving birth, when there is no help or equipment to hand.

This third book of 'MUMs Recipes' will raise even more much needed funds to make greater progress and bring hope and happiness to many women and their families in Malawi.

Sarah Brown is Global Patron of the White Ribbon Alliance for Safe Motherhood and closely involved with the Maternal Mortality campaign to reduce the number of maternal deaths around the world. She is Co-Chair of the Leadership Group on Maternal Mortality, alongside Bience Gawanas, Social Affairs Commissioner at the African Union and they are working on a campaign in Africa to engage country leaders, First Ladies and other officials to champion their cause. She is married to the UK Prime Minister, Gordon Brown.

INTRODUCTION

Thank you for buying this, the third and the last MUMs Recipe Book. If this is the first MUMs book you have bought, you should know that MUMs is about helping Malawi's Underprivileged Mothers and about sharing the joy of cooking.

The advantage of being a small charity and having a finger on the pulse is that we can help individuals in small, but significant, ways. For example, over these last six months, while I was in Malawi, I was in a position to feed young malnourished and hungry children, many of whom were children and orphans born in Bwaila Hospital. Two feeding stations were set up in April 2009 and MUMs is now feeding 200 needy pre-school children three times a week. It is in identifying such problems at point of need and acting upon them - in addition to raising funds for major capital projects, such as the new maternity wing at Bwaila - that MUMs is proving most useful.
(For more information on the difference your money has made, go to www.mumsrecipes.org)

People often ask me where I get the energy and the enthusiasm for the MUMs project. The answer is very simple. Carol Craig, Chief Executive at the Centre for Confidence and Well-Being in Glasgow, put as the first of her Ten Steps to Happiness, "Do something meaningful or worthwhile – something where the achievement is not just about you but serves a larger goal." Whatever energy I have given to MUMs has been repaid many times over with the pleasure and the sense of achievement I have felt. It has for example been a real privilege to be able to share a little of the lives of many wonderful Malawian women. When I am with them, I feel humbled by their resilience and their gentleness; when I leave them, I feel exhilarated by the strength of their spirit. It was therefore important to me that this book shares something of the warmth I feel for Malawi and its people – a warmth Sally has captured in her drawings. Yes, the MUMs journey has been an amazing one for Iain and for me and one we couldn't have done without lots of support from other people – other people who also know about Step One! That is why MUMs Three is a book of recipes from friends.

Linda McDonald

"If we are lucky, we will suffer a taste of powerlessness in our own private lives. Because then things change. Then we begin to see with a gentler, broader vision and talk with a kinder tongue and feel with deeper feelings for those with whom powerlessness is a way of life." **Joan Chittister.**

For my wonderful husband Iain,
who has been by my side every step of the way.

TO AN UNBORN GRANDCHILD

I picture you curled up in the dark
Knowing only the pulse of blood,
bump of bone and rib, your mother's
heartbeat. Have you all your toes now?
Are your eyelashes in place?

Get your head down. The head
is always troublesome.
After that it's slither and slide,
blood, mucus, love.

Come easily. Come swiftly.
Come with everything right about you.
Come with a wonderful mix of genes
that takes the best from all of us.

The air will be shocking, I know,
but take a deep breath.
Tell us you've arrived. Cry.

'To An Unborn Grandchild' was written when my daughter, Kate was pregnant
with her first child. A boy - now 5! - *Diana Hendry*

From: Late Love & Other Whodunits (Peterloo/Mariscat Press) by **Diana Hendry**

ACKNOWLEDGEMENTS

Writing acknowledgements always makes me appreciate how very lucky I've been in the support MUMs has had. I've previously acknowledged many of the following for their help with MUMs One and Two, but there are always new faces to thank. So, for their many and various contributions, I'd like to thank all the friends of MUMs for their recipes – and Craigie's Farm for its special section; Sally for her drawings – and for the time she gave to make them as fine as they are; Lara Meguid for her own sensitive drawing; and Diana Hendry for allowing the republication of her affecting poems about childbirth. I'd like to thank Sarah Brown for her generous introduction and for her continued support of MUMs and also for her encouragement and friendship.

Donna, Bruce and Charlotte at Smart Design and Print are responsible for the production of the book you hold in your hands. But without Lorna Pascall, giving untold hours of her close reading, fine tuning skills, none of the MUMs Recipe books, book three included, would be as useful as I hope they are.

I am blessed with wonderful, supportive friends and a loving extended family. But it's my immediate family, Katie, Sally and Iain to whom I am most thankful. None of them has ever questioned my involvement in MUMs or my desire to spend time in Malawi. Katie's and Sally's loving independence is, I think, remarkable, as is the steadfast support of Iain: my deepest gratitude to all three of them.

COCKTAILS & CANAPÉS

I have included this section to share with you our annual cocktail party which we have between Christmas and New Year. The best part of this party is that the invitation is from 6pm till 8pm only, so apart from the cocktails running out and the mixtures becoming 'whatever is left' it also means that, as the hostess, you are off shift at 8ish.

The canapés are easy and prepared ahead which is a must, so you can be the one to open the door to your guests. Also being ahead of the game allows the party to end up in a tidy kitchen, as many good parties do.

Included in this section are canapés which I learnt to make while I was in Malawi.

SANGRIA

I had this at a ladies charity lunch and loved it. I have tried to make sangria before and it never quite tasted like the local version I drink on holiday. But then again the sun, sand and smells of Spain were missing!

The alcohol, sugar and lemonade quantities can be adjusted as desired.

Ingredients:
1 bottle red wine
chunks of fruit eg orange, lemon, apple
2 tbsp sugar
1 or 2 measures of alcohol eg vodka, martini, brandy etc
lemonade

Method:
1. Mix everything together in a large jug except the lemonade, this can be done well in advance and left to stand.
2. ½ an hour before required, add the lemonade to taste.
3. Serve with ice.

COCKTAILS

Measurements below are approximate and can be adjusted according to preferences. A shot is 25ml. Each recipe is for one drink.

Cosmopolitan
1 shot Vodka
½ shot Cointreau
½ shot cranberry juice

Shake all ingredients with ice and strain into a chilled martini glass.

Tequila Collins
2 shots Tequila
juice of ½ lemon
ice
1 tsp icing sugar
soda water

Shake together and pour into glasses where the rim has been dipped in egg white and then salt.

Mudslide
2 shots Baileys
1 shot Vodka
1 scoop vanilla ice cream

Liquidise and serve.

Peach Daiquiri (or strawberry)
peaches or strawberries, fresh or tinned
1 shot White Rum
2 tsp lime juice
1 tsp sugar
crushed ice

Liquidise and serve.

Christmas Cocktail
dash of Cointreau to give a kick
Bubbly
cranberry juice

Mix together and serve in cocktail glasses.

SALMON AND PRAWN FLATBREADS
These are a taste of the canapés I use for parties.

Method:
1. Warm 2 packs of garlic flatbreads according to packet instructions, then cut into bite size pieces.
2. Top with generous dollops of smoked salmon pâté, either bought or using the recipe in MUMs Recipes Book Two, page 14, which works beautifully.
3. Top with a prawn and some snipped salad cress to decorate.

GAMEY SAUSAGE ROLLS
(Makes about 12-16)
These are good around Christmas because you use game sausages and can be made ahead.

Method:
1. Preheat the oven to 200ºC or Gas Mark 6.
2. Cut a 375g packet of ready rolled puff pastry in half lengthways.
3. Remove the skins from 6-8 venison or wild boar sausages and place half of them in a line just off centre on the first strip of pastry.
4. Brush one edge with beaten egg, fold over the pastry and press to stick. Cut into 6 or 8 rolls.
5. Place on baking sheet, brush with egg and make little cuts in the top.
6. Repeat with remaining pastry then bake for 12-15 minutes until browned and risen.

In Malawi it is quite normal to be invited to someone's house for a 'sundowner'. This is a wonderful term for drinks and nibbles at around 5 o'clock to watch the warm, red African sun disappear below the horizon. Next time you have friends for a drink in the summer ask them to come for a 'sundowner'.

These three recipes were devised and made by Philip, who is cook to the Irish Ambassador. I had them at a reception in the residence on St Patrick's Day. One afternoon I spent a most enjoyable few hours watching and learning as Philip showed me how to make the recipes. He was assisted by the lovely Sarah who cut and prepared the vegetables and tidied up.

CHICKEN SATAY
(Serves about 20, after breaking each skewer in half)

Ingredients:
6 chicken breasts, cubed
skewers

Marinade:
1 onion
4 garlic cloves
3 tbsp soya sauce
1 tsp oyster sauce
3 tsp honey
3 tbsp olive oil
2 tbsp fresh coriander

Satay Sauce:
1 small jar peanut butter
1 tbsp soya sauce
2.5cm/1" piece fresh ginger, grated
4 tbsp brown sugar, dissolved in a little hot water

Method:
For marinade:
1. Liquidise all the ingredients for marinade, add pinch of salt and pepper.
2. Marinade chicken overnight.
3. Put about 5 pieces of chicken on each skewer.
4. Heat a little oil in a frying pan and cook, turning until chicken is cooked. Keep warm in oven - up to an hour before serving.

For sauce:
1. Mix together in bowl., adding more water if necessary.
2. Serve along with chicken as a dipping sauce.

MEATBALLS

(Makes about 120)

It is worth making this large amount because they freeze so well. Remember to use fresh mince if you are going to freeze them. Obviously Philip uses large quantities because the Ambassador's wife plans a lot of receptions, but in this case it is a good idea to follow the recipe for the amounts.

Ingredients:

3kg/6½lb fresh steak mince
1½ tsp salt
½ tsp paprika
½ tsp ground black pepper
a sprinkling of peri-peri or hot chilli powder
2 pinches nutmeg
¼ beef stock cube, crumbled
1 tsp mixed herbs
2 tbsp white wine
7 cloves garlic, crushed
1 big green pepper, chopped
2 onions, chopped
1 tbsp fresh coriander or parsley
2 eggs
½ - 1 cup dried breadcrumbs (see Accompaniments chapter)

For sauce:
2 tbsp sweet chilli sauce
1 tbsp tomato ketchup

Method:

1. Mix all the ingredients together and make into balls whatever size you want - I think about enough for 2 bites so a little bigger than a teaspoon.
2. Lay them on trays and either cook them fresh in the oven at 200°C, Gas Mark 6, for 20 minutes or open freeze, and put in zip lock bags for another time.
3. If cooking from frozen, cook at 200°C, Gas Mark 6, for 30 minutes.
4. Put on cocktail sticks and serve with sauce.
5. To make sauce mix the sweet chilli sauce with the tomato ketchup.

MINI QUICHE
(Makes 30)
A great way to use up any left-overs in the fridge.

Ingredients:
1 cup plain flour
175g/6oz margarine
1 egg
mixed milk and water

Filling:
½ cup double cream
1 cup of milk
3 eggs, beaten
salt and pepper
broccoli, cooked, left small
cheese, grated
tomato, diced small
green pepper, diced small
fried onion, diced small

Method:
1. Preheat oven to 180°C, Gas Mark 4.
2. Rub fat into flour and add the egg mixed with milk and water to bind together.
3. Roll out on a floured board (no need to chill or bake blind) and cut using a small size glass as a cutter. Line a small bun tin with pastry circles.
4. Mix cream, milk and egg in a jug.
5. Fill the quiches with your chosen vegetables. Top up with the egg mixture and sprinkle with extra cheese on top.
6. Cook till golden in colour and the mixture has set, approx 20 minutes.

CAMEMBERT BREAD
I saw this in an old American cookbook and loved the difference from normal garlic bread.

Ingredients:
225g/8oz round Camembert cheese
225g/8oz butter, softened
1 tsp garlic powder
4 tbsp fresh parsley, chopped
1 long French stick
parmesan cheese, freshly grated

Method:
1. Combine Camembert, butter, garlic powder and 3 tbsp parsley in food processor until smooth.
2. Slice the bread and spread the processed mixture between all slices and along the top of the loaf.
3. Sprinkle the top with remaining parsley and parmesan.
4. Wrap loaf in foil and bake at 180°C, Gas Mark 4 for 40 minutes.

MAPLE, SESAME AND MUSTARD SAUSAGES
Make plenty!

Method:
1. Bake cocktail sausages in the oven until cooked through and browned.
2. Toss through some grain mustard, maple syrup and sesame seeds.
3. Return the sausages to the oven for a further 5 minutes.

TRIPLE DECKER DIP
Lorna first made this years ago. What was lovely apart from the taste, was serving it in a small glass dish that showed the three contrasting layers beautifully. If you want to cheat use a tub of guacamole, salsa and a tub of sour cream and chive dip from the supermarket.

Ingredients:
½ cup avocado mashed with 1 tsp lemon juice
½ cup salsa (recipes in Accompaniments chapter)
½ cup spring onions, chopped
½ cup sour cream

To decorate:
½ cup mature coloured cheddar cheese, grated
1 tomato, chopped
a few black olives, chopped

Method:
1. Mix the green onions with the sour cream.
2. Layer each ingredient in a glass serving bowl in the order given.
3. Decorate with the cheese, tomato and olives.
4. Serve with crackers or tortillas for dipping.

MINI MERINGUE BITES
It is always appreciated having a sweet canapé at a party along with the savoury and these will disappear.

Method:
1. Make meringues using the recipe from MUMs Recipes Book One on page 51. Instead of using a soup spoon to shape the meringue use a teaspoon, you are only wanting a bite size to eat when they are cooked.
2. Store in an airtight container until needed.
3. To serve, whip up some double cream and put a blob on each meringue, topped with a raspberry or strawberry.

"Looking at the new Bwaila and Ethel Mutharika Maternity Units I almost feel a miracle has happened, especially considering that it all started with 'little people'. But on reflection the new buildings are a testimony to the fact that there are no 'little people' and the least 'little' are the women who give birth here and their children whose first impression of the world will be of these beautiful hospitals."

Dr Tarek Meguid
Consultant Obstetrician at Bwaila and Ethel Mutharika Maternity Hospitals.

Simple Soups

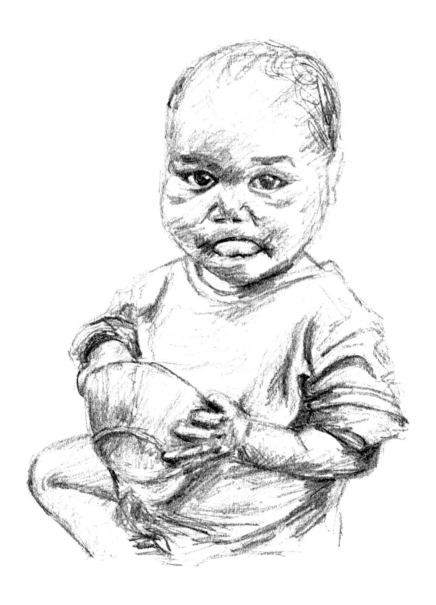

CULLEN SKINK

(Serves 4)

I found this old Scottish cooking book in the National Trust for Scotland shop in Brodick Castle on the island of Arran a number of years ago and didn't use any of the recipes until I got married and now we have the Cullen Skink often with some crusty bread and what is left Roy shares with his friends when he goes shooting. – *Gillian Smith*

Ingredients:
1 piece smoked haddock
1 leek, chopped
1 potato, peeled and diced
2 tbsp butter
1 tbsp flour
300ml/½ pint water
300ml/½ pint milk
parsley
bay leaf

Method:
1. Melt 1 tbsp of the butter and soften the leeks in it.
2. Add the haddock in small pieces, the potato, bay leaf, milk and water.
3. Bring to the boil and simmer for 20 minutes.
4. Mix the remaining 1 tbsp of butter and flour together with a fork and then add to the liquid, stirring to prevent lumps.
5. Bring to the boil, add salt and pepper, scatter chopped parsley over and serve.

DOREEN'S LENTIL SOUP

(Serves 6-8)

I was looking for more soup recipes when visiting my neighbour Doreen's home one day. Her husband Stewart was in the garden about to have his lunch and raved about this soup she was about to dish up. That was a good enough recommendation from the man of the house! So here it is.

Ingredients:
1.8 litres/3 pints of stock made with 4 ham cubes
7 tbsp lentils
2 carrots, peeled and chopped
1 large onion, peeled and chopped
a few slices of bacon or ham, optional
a little butter

Method:
1. Melt butter in a large pan and sauté onion, carrot and bacon if using for a few minutes.
2. Add lentils and stock and simmer for approximately 30 minutes.
3. Serve in warm bowls. As with most soups they are better the next day. Can be frozen.

GLYNDA'S CARROT AND ORANGE SOUP

(Serves 4-6)

Delicious! Takes five minutes to prepare, 20 minutes to cook and looks and tastes superb!
- *Glynda Kennedy*

Ingredients:
25g/1oz butter
450g/1lb carrots, peeled and chopped
1 large onion, chopped
1 large orange, flesh without pith or membrane
finely grated zest of ½ the orange
600ml/1 pint vegetable stock
150ml/¼ pint pure orange juice – must be <u>pure</u>, not made from concentrate
salt and pepper

Method:
1. Sweat off the onions in butter.
2. Add carrots.
3. Add zest of ½ the orange together with the flesh of the orange.
4. Add stock and orange juice.
5. Cook until carrots are soft, about 20 minutes.
6. Liquidise and season. Add more stock and juice if necessary for the desired consistency.
7. Serve with a swirl of double cream, chopped parsley and walnut bread.

JANE'S SOUP

(Serves 6)

**Given to me by my mother - a firm favourite with the family and friends. Delicious flavour.
My girls live on it on winter days and if a fresh batch is not there when they come in from
school there is always some in the freezer!** – *Jane Arnot*

Ingredients:
55g/2oz butter
560g/1lb 4oz tomatoes, chopped
1 onion, chopped
1 carrot, chopped
1 stick celery, chopped
600ml/1 pint stock
bouquet garni
salt and pepper
25g/1oz flour
300ml/½ pint milk
4 dessertspoons cream

Method:
1. Sauté the vegetables in 25g/1oz butter.
2. Add the stock and bouquet garni.
3. Simmer for 15-20 minutes till soft.
4. Blend.
5. Make a roux with the other 25g/1oz butter, the flour and milk – you want a thin consistency.
6. Add the purée and the cream and blend again if necessary. Serve.

HEARTY VEGETABLE SOUP

(Serves at least 6)

My first boyfriend's mum taught me this recipe. She was lovely, so kind to me and taught me a lot. She very sadly died from cancer but I think of her every time I make it.

I met Linda on a Comic Relief trip to Malawi, Sarah Brown had told me to find her. She talked about Linda in such glowing terms, I couldn't wait to meet her. When I did meet her I wasn't disappointed. She was everything I'd hoped for....such energy and passion and she's single handedly responsible for changing thousands of women's lives in Malawi. Well done Linda!! – *Davina McColl*

Ingredients:

1 large onion, chopped
1 large red pepper, chopped
2 large handfuls of button mushrooms, cut in half
3 large sweet potatoes, cut into cubes
3 sticks celery, chopped
3 large carrots, chopped
½ cauliflower, cut into pieces
1 large broccoli head, cut into small florets
2 tbsp tomato paste
1 chicken stock cube (or fresh chicken stock)

Method:

1. Sauté the onion and peppers in olive oil till soft then add all the other ingredients and stir.
2. Keep stirring, add salt, pepper and the tomato paste. Stir until everything has a bit of paste. Don't let it burn!!!!
3. Cover with water and a chicken stock cube (or fresh chicken stock) and bring to the boil.
4. Simmer until all the vegetables are soft. Season to taste. I like to mash it up a bit but it's up to you!
5. I serve with crusty garlic bread and a healthy dollop of grated red Leicester cheese on top!! Yummy!

LENTIL AND CARROT SOUP
(Serves 12)
This is a great soup to make for large numbers. Real ham must be used to give it flavour.

Ingredients:
1 ham hock
1 large leek, washed, peeled and chopped
2 large onions, chopped
450g/1lb carrots, chopped
450g/1lb lentils, washed
175g/6oz rice
400g tin tomatoes
2.7 litres/4½ pints water

Method:
You will need a large pot.
1. Simmer the ham hock for 1½ hours.
2. Put the leek, onions, carrots, rice and lentils into the pan with the ham and cook for a further 15 minutes or until the vegetables are cooked.
3. Remove the ham from pan and keep to use for a meal later.
4. Place the cooked leek, onions, carrots, rice and lentils into a liquidiser and add the tomatoes.
5. Liquidise until the mixture is smooth.
6. Return the mixture to pot and simmer for 5-10 minutes.
7. Add salt and pepper to taste and serve in a hot bowl.

POTAGE BONNE FEMME
(Serves 6)

Ingredients:
450g/1lb potatoes, peeled and chopped
3 carrots, peeled and chopped
2 large leeks, sliced
40g/1½oz butter
1.2 litres/2 pints stock
salt
sugar
cream parsley, chopped

Method:
1. Melt butter in pan, add leeks and carrots.
2. Let them get thoroughly hot and saturated with the butter then add potatoes, stock, a little salt and a lump or two of sugar.
3. Cook steadily (but not at a gallop) for 25-30 minutes.
4. Liquidise when ready to serve.
5. Add the cream and parsley.

PEA AND MINT SOUP
(Serves 6)
Lovely soup!

Ingredients:
55g/2oz butter
225g/8oz onions, sliced
110g/4oz lettuce, trimmed and chopped
450g/1lb frozen peas
1 heaped tsp dried mint **or** 2 heaped tsp chopped fresh mint
55g/2oz petits pois
salt and pepper

To serve:
whipped cream
fresh mint

Method:
1. Melt the butter and add the onion. Cook gently until the onion is softened but not brown.
2. Add the lettuce leaves, stir and add 300ml/10fl oz of water, simmer for 40 minutes.
3. Liquidise until smooth, set aside.
4. Place the peas in the same pan and cover with 300ml/10fl oz water and bring to the boil as quickly as possible. As soon as the water comes to the boil remove from the heat, add the mint and liquidise until smooth. Add to the onion and lettuce mixture and stir.
5. Season and add water if necessary – it should not be too thin.
6. When ready to serve, return to pan and reheat soup. Add the petits pois. Do not allow the soup to boil for more than a minute or two as it will change colour.
7. Serve in warmed bowls garnished with a little whipped cream and fresh mint.

LADIES WHO LUNCH

CAULIFLOWER CHEESE
(Serves 2-4)
I love cauliflower cheese and it is brilliant served with most savoury things – nice steamed vegetables, alongside a roast, or with some cold cuts. It is also very adjustable to suit most dietary requirements (no dairy, no wheat, whatever). - *Sarah Brown*

Ingredients:
a lovely, preferably organic cauliflower, cut into quarters
25g/1oz butter or Pure margarine (non-dairy)
25g/1oz plain flour (or cornflour)
300ml/ ½ pint milk (any milk, full fat, half fat or skimmed; goat's milk or soya milk also work well)
a bay leaf
175-225g/6-8oz mature cheddar cheese, grated
a pinch of salt (and ground black pepper if you like the taste, I tend to leave it out as it is easy to add later)

Method:
1. Put on the kettle and get out a large saucepan. Put the cauliflower in the pan with some of the green leaves still on. Add boiling water and put on the hob to cook for 10-15 minutes (or until it is soft to touch with a knife – try not to over cook so it goes mushy).
2. While the cauliflower is cooking, get out a medium saucepan and arm yourself with a nice long handled wooden spoon.
3. Add the butter/margarine to the pan and melt on the hob (obviously keeping well away from your boiling cauliflower pan).
4. Add the flour and stir in to the melted butter/margarine until properly mixed and let it cook for a minute.
5. Add the milk slowly (and the bay leaf) and keep stirring so you don't get big floury lumps. You should get a nice smooth sauce. If it all goes horribly wrong this can be sorted out quickly with a hand whisk (the best ones are those little wooden handled ones). Keep stirring (or whisking) until the sauce starts to boil and the sauce will thicken. At this point turn off the heat. Now add the pinch of salt and half the grated cheese and stir it in.
6. Your cauliflower should just be done by this time. Drain and leave in the colander for a moment to let the water run through properly.
7. Turn on your grill.
8. Turn the cauliflower out of the pan into a nice big open dish. Pour the cheese sauce over the top. Scatter the second half of the grated cheese across the top. If you spot the bay leaf you can hoik this out at this point, but not a disaster if you never do.
9. Now you can grill your lovely dish until the cheese on top has melted and just starts to brown. Best served immediately.

CHICKPEA AND MANGO SALAD

My sister-in-law made this winning salad for a summer party in her Surrey garden. She kindly gave me the recipe and I've been copying it out for other people who enjoy it ever since! – *Ali Brown*

Ingredients:
3 x 400g tins chickpeas
1 red onion, chopped
1 large ripe mango or 1 tin, chopped
1 apple, chopped
1 tbsp mint, chopped
1 tbsp fresh coriander, chopped

For dressing:
180ml/6fl oz natural yoghurt
3 tsp mango chutney
1 garlic clove, crushed
2 tsp curry powder
1 tbsp lime juice

Method:
1. Mix all salad ingredients in a large bowl.
2. Prepare dressing and combine with chickpea mix.

GOAT'S CHEESE AND BUTTERNUT SQUASH FLAN
(Serves 6)

You can use any strong melting cheese, lovely with a simple green salad.

Ingredients:
500g pkt shortcrust pastry
1 small butternut squash
1 red onion, chopped roughly
4 garlic cloves, unpeeled
1 tbsp thyme
100g pkt soft goat's cheese
150g pkt goat's cheese with rind

Method:
1. Preheat oven to 190°C, Gas Mark 5.
2. Roll out pastry to 3mm/1/8" thickness. Line a 23cm/9" round flan tin and bake blind for 15 minutes.
3. Cut the squash into chunks and remove skin and seeds. Drizzle with olive oil, season and put in roasting tin with onion, garlic and thyme. Roast for 20 minutes until the squash is cooked.
4. Spread the soft goat's cheese on the bottom of the flan case. Squeeze the garlic from its skin and mash with ½ the squash. Spread over the base. Season and scatter over the onion and remaining squash.
5. Slice goat's cheese with rind into rounds and place on top.
6. Bake for 20-30 minutes.

HOT SMOKED SALMON AND AVOCADO ON A SWEET PEPPER SALAD, WITH A LEMON AND CHILLI DRESSING

(Serves 8 for a starter)

Prepare the dressing ahead of time. Put everything together a few hours before you need it. I always put a disc of Bakewell paper at the bottom of the mould – to make for easy removal.

Ingredients:
4 medium fillets of ready hot smoked salmon, or ready flaked
2 large avocados
125g/4½oz mayonnaise and 125g/4½oz crème fraîche **or** 250g/9oz crème fraîche

For the salad:
1 red pepper, roasted, skinned and sliced
1 yellow pepper, roasted, skinned and sliced
1 handful of rocket
1 handful of lamb's lettuce

For the vinaigrette:
1 grated lemon rind and juice
1 pinch saffron
1 tsp lemon oil, optional
6 tbsp olive oil
3 tbsp white wine vinegar
1 red chilli, deseeded and finely chopped or chilli powder to taste
salt and pepper

Method:
1. Roughly flake the salmon then mix with half the mayonnaise and crème fraîche mixture and season. Put to one side.
2. To make the vinaigrette, mix all ingredients together.
3. Peel and dice the avocado and mix with the remainder of the mayonnaise and crème fraîche mixture.
4. Take an individual mould (ie dariole or similar) and layer salmon and avocado. Chill in fridge for a couple of hours.

To serve:
1. Toss the salad ingredients together with a little of the vinaigrette.
2. Place in the middle of the 8 plates, and turn out moulds on top of salad.
3. Finally drizzle some more lemon and chilli vinaigrette around the dish.
4. Serve with brown bread.

HONEY CHICKEN AND BACON SALAD

(Serves 4)

I sometimes omit the chicken if the salad is to be an accompaniment. - *Anne Gaskell*

Ingredients:
450g/1lb new potatoes, scrubbed
175g/6oz fine green beans, trimmed
6 rashers rindless streaky bacon
120g bag mixed salad leaves
4 roasted chicken breasts cut into chunks or about 700g/1lb 9oz cooked chicken
150ml/¼ pint bought honey and mustard dressing

Method:
1. Cook potatoes for 8-10 minutes then add beans to water and cook a further 3 minutes till just tender. Drain and rinse under cold water to cool completely.
2. Cut potatoes into quarters lengthways.
3. Grill the bacon till crisp. Cool and break into small pieces.
4. Scatter salad leaves on platter.
5. Toss the chicken with the green beans and potatoes and as much of the dressing as you require then spoon over the salad leaves. Scatter crispy bacon over the top and serve.

QUESADILLAS

These are great for a fun meal. Anything goes in the middle but cheese is a must to help stick the tortilla together.

Ingredients per wrap:
tortilla wrap
2 slices parma ham (or wafer thin ham, or chicken)
2 tbsp cheddar, grated
1 tbsp jalapeno jelly (recipe in Accompaniments chapter)
1 tbsp coriander
olive oil spray

To serve:
Salsa (recipes in Accompaniments chapter)

Method:
1. Spread jalapeno jelly over half of the wrap and place a slice of parma ham on top followed by cheese, coriander and the other slice of ham.
2. Fold the wrap in half and spray both sides with olive oil.
3. Heat a ridged griddle pan and when hot place the now semi circular wrap on the griddle for a minute on each side.
4. Transfer to a chopping board to cut into wedge shaped slices.

TOULA'S TZATZIKI

This recipe was given to Sue by the people whose apartment she rented while on a family holiday in Kefalonia in 1994. They were invited to a birthday party with wonderful food and great dancing. Sue asked Toula for this recipe and uses it often – a great reminder of lovely people and a fabby holiday.

Ingredients:
1 cucumber, grated and the water <u>well squeezed out</u>. Use a colander if you have one!
2-3 garlic cloves, crushed
salt
1 dessert spoon olive oil
250g/9oz Greek yogurt

Mix together and enjoy with Spanokopita overleaf.
Great as part of a cold buffet or with kebabs or salmon.

SPANAKOPITA (Greek spinach and Feta cheese pie)
(Serves 6)

Heather served this at a girls night. She lived in Greece for several years and has fond memories of eating this on the beach!

Ingredients:
75ml/2½ fl oz olive oil (preferably Greek!)
1 large onion, diced
2 garlic cloves, crushed
400g/14oz spinach, washed (easier to buy ready washed packs from the supermarket)
25g/1oz parsley, chopped
2 eggs, lightly whisked
400g/14oz Feta cheese
¼ tsp nutmeg
8 sheets Filo pastry (shortcrust pastry also very good)
salt and pepper

Method:
1. Preheat the oven to 175°C, Gas Mark 3.
2. Cook spinach in packet in microwave according to instructions. Place cooked spinach in a sieve over sink in order to drain as much fluid out as possible. Periodically return and press down with a spoon to squeeze it.
3. Cook onion, parsley and garlic in a little of the olive oil until soft then allow to cool.
4. In a large bowl, mix the eggs and Feta cheese together (Feta should be in large enough lumps to taste) till well mixed together. Add the onion mixture, nutmeg, salt and pepper and mix.
5. When all fluid is out of spinach, add to bowl and mix up well.
6. Take a round loose bottom tin (21cm/8") and line with filo, brush the first sheet of filo with olive oil and place face down in tin leaving some over the edge. Turn the baking tin 45 degrees and repeat, continue till all the tin is covered.
7. Fill tin with the spinach/Feta mixture and fold over the hanging filo.
8. Seal top with the remaining filo and brush top with olive oil.
9. Bake for 35 minutes until golden brown and serve warm with a classic Greek salad and tzatziki (see previous page for recipe).

TARTIFLETTE
(Serves 4)

Reblochon is quite a strong-flavoured cheese. You can serve this dish with a sliced apple. I tend not to season too much because of the saltiness of the bacon and cheese. – *Corinne Duncan*

Ingredients:
225g/8oz Reblochon cheese
675g/1½ lb potatoes
1 onion, chopped
1 clove garlic, chopped
300ml/½ pint crème fraîche
125g pancetta (or 3-4 rashers back bacon, chopped)

Method:

1. Preheat the oven to 200°C, Gas Mark 6.
2. Parboil the potatoes. They should still be hard enough for you to slice without them breaking up.
3. Fry the onion and garlic in a little oil, add the pancetta (or bacon).
4. In a gratin dish, put a layer of potato slices, followed by a layer of the pancetta/onion, a bit of crème fraîche, a layer of sliced Reblochon (the outside layer is a bit hard but edible).
5. Repeat the process and finish with a layer of Reblochon.
6. Put the dish in the oven until the cheese has melted and starts to take colour (a proper gratin) – about 30 minutes.

TORTILLA DE PATATA

(Serves 8)

This traditional Spanish omelette must be cooked in a non stick pan otherwise you will end up with a fried scrambled egg and potato mush! I have a special pan that is strictly used for cooking tortillas in. You also need a large serving plate that must be the same size or bigger than the frying pan as it will be used for turning the tortilla during cooking. I learned early on in my life in Spain to make a good tortilla. – *Rachel Macleod*

Ingredients:

5 large potatoes
5 large eggs
olive oil
salt

Method:

1. Cover the bottom of frying pan with olive oil at least 1cm deep.
2. Peel and cut the potatoes into small pieces or slices.
3. Break the eggs into a bowl and whisk.... throw in salt.
4. Heat olive oil and throw in prepared potatoes, cook until soft, turning regularly. Try not to brown too much.
5. Salt potatoes to taste.
6. Without removing from heat pour egg mixture on top of cooked potatoes.
7. Cook for a few minutes and when judging base of tortilla to be slightly firm place large plate on top and turn onto plate.
8. Immediately slide tortilla back into hot pan to allow the other side to cook. You can do this several times.
9. The tortilla should become a golden brown, not burnt, but the inside should be cooked and not sloppy. This will be achieved by turning the tortilla several times onto the plate and back into the pan.
10. The tortilla tastes much better if left for a while to cool.

There are many versions you can experiment with eg. onion, green peppers or other vegetables. These you can cook with or before the potatoes, then follow the same instructions. If you decide to use cheese it is best grated and mixed into the egg mixture before pouring over the potatoes. However the original and the best is still the potato only version!

Very useful for suppers with a crispy salad and also great for picnics as it is equally yummy served cold with a selection of meats and cheeses. For a filling, nourishing and hugely fattening 'almuerzo', make yourself a 'bocadillo de tortilla de patata'. Serve the Spanish way with half a loaf of crusty bread stick opened and softened with olive oil and tomato.

WINTER SLAW

(Serves 8)

Liked the sound of all the ingredients and it works.

Ingredients:

4 large carrots, peeled and coarsely grated
½ red onion, very finely sliced
½ red cabbage, finely sliced or shredded
2 apples, peeled, cored, finely sliced and tossed in juice of ½ lemon
150g/5½oz sultanas
55g/2oz toasted pinenuts

For the dressing:
3 tbsp Greek yogurt
3 tbsp crème fraîche
juice of 2 lemons
1½ tbsp Dijon mustard

Method:

1. Put the carrot in a colander and squeeze out any excess moisture.
2. Put the carrot, red onion, cabbage, apple, sultanas and half of the pinenuts into a large mixing bowl and toss together.
3. To make the dressing, combine all the ingredients in a bowl and pour over the slaw. Season and toss, ensuring all the dressing is distributed.
4. Pour into a bowl and sprinkle with remaining pinenuts.

YIA-YIA'S SPANAKOPITA (Greek spinach and cheese pie)

(Serves 4-6 as starter)

This is a favourite of ours. Yia Yia, my mother-in-law, is Greek and she has handed this recipe down to my daughters so they do not lose their Greek ancestry. – *Rona Ferguson*

Ingredients:

500g/1lb 2oz frozen spinach
1 large onion, finely chopped
2 eggs, beaten
225g/8oz strong cheese, grated (ideally ½ Feta and ½ strong white cheddar)
1 tbsp parsley, chopped
110g/4oz butter, melted (for brushing pan and pastry)
1 pkt frozen puff pastry

Method:

1. Preheat oven to 200°C, Gas Mark 6.
2. Gently fry the onion in a little butter.
3. Add frozen spinach and fry with onion until melted down.
4. Add cheese, parsley and 2 beaten eggs. Fry for a couple of minutes.
5. Allow mixture to cool.
6. Grease a baking tin with butter.
7. Roll out ½ the puff pastry. Place in baking tin then grease pastry with butter.
8. Pour mixture on top of pastry.
9. Roll out remainder of puff pastry and place on top of spinach mixture.
10. Brush top with melted butter.
11. Cut pastry into squares and bake in a hot oven until top is brown.

PROMISING PASTAS

CHICKEN AND SPINACH LASAGNE

(Serves 4/5)

Lunch time in a school staff room can provide just enough time for sharing of recipes! My friends, Anne and Lorraine invented and reinvented this one. Both are used to cooking for large numbers at the drop of a hat and depending on time available you can cheat by using bought cheese sauce and a jar of Lloyd Grossman Tomato and Chilli pasta sauce. I especially like the fact that the spinach goes in raw. - *Lorna Pascall*

Ingredients:
4 chicken breasts, chopped
1 garlic clove, chopped
1 large onion, chopped
1 red chilli, chopped
2 x 400g tins chopped tomatoes
250g bag baby spinach
450ml/16fl oz white sauce
250g pkt fresh lasagne
110g/4oz cheddar cheese, grated

Method:
1. Preheat oven to 180°C, Gas Mark 4.
2. Brown the chicken.
3. Add the onion, garlic, chilli and tomatoes.
4. Simmer with the lid off for approximately 15 minutes.
5. Using a lasagne dish 20cm x 30cm/8" x 12" start layering the lasagne with fresh lasagne followed by the tomato chicken mixture, then the uncooked spinach and a good drizzle of white sauce. Repeat the layers and cover the top with white sauce.
6. Sprinkle generously with grated cheese.
7. Bake in the oven for 35 minutes.

GOAT'S CHEESE AND TOMATO CANNELLONI

(Serves 4)

This is great for tomato growers who are looking for ways of using up a glut of the crop.

Ingredients:
2 tbsp olive oil
1kg/2lb 4oz ripe cherry tomatoes, cut in half
2 tsp dried oregano
2 tsp sugar
200g/7oz soft rindless goat's cheese
6 tbsp fresh red or green pesto
250g pkt fresh lasagne sheets
350g/12oz ripe vine tomatoes, roughly chopped
50g/1¾oz parmesan, freshly grated

To serve:
basil leaves and green salad

Method:
1. Preheat oven to 220°C, Gas Mark 7.
2. Lightly grease a 25cm x 25cm/ 10" x 10" baking dish.
3. Set aside 225g/8oz of the cherry tomatoes for the topping.
4. Heat the oil in a frying pan, add remaining cherry tomatoes and cover tightly. Cook over a high heat, shaking the pan occasionally, for 5 minutes until the tomatoes start to break down. Stir in the oregano, sugar, salt and pepper.
5. In a bowl, soften the cheese with a fork and mix in the pesto. Cut the lasagne sheets in half and spread the cheese mixture over. Divide the chopped vine tomatoes between each sheet and roll up.(Don't worry if they crack)
6. Spoon half the tomato sauce over the base of the dish. Arrange the pasta rolls on top, then spoon over the remaining sauce. Scatter the reserved cherry tomato halves on top and cover with foil.
7. Bake for 30 minutes. Uncover, sprinkle with the parmesan and bake for a further 10 minutes until starting to brown. Allow to stand for 5 minutes before serving.
8. Scatter with basil leaves and serve with a green salad.

GARLIC PRAWNS WITH CONCHIGLE
(Serves 4)

This was an old favourite before I lost my hands to meningitis. It has been made by many family members with many substitutions, additions and different kinds of pasta - but this is the best version. I wondered if I would be able to make it again when I got out of hospital without hands - because grating ginger and finely chopping garlic aren't the easiest things. Then I discovered jars of pre-chopped ginger and garlic - and it couldn't be easier. (I just miss out the lemon rind and rely on the juice!) - *Olivia Giles*

Ingredients:
350g/12oz pasta shells
55g/2oz butter
4 cloves garlic, peeled and crushed
2 tbsp root ginger, finely chopped
2 tbsp milk
grated rind and juice of ½ a small lemon
1 pkt coriander - or as much as you like really
450g/1lb prawns (defrosted from frozen is fine but dry them well)
(you can substitute chicken and fry it gently to cook through before you fry the garlic and ginger)
2 avocados, firm, ripe and chopped into chunks
salt and freshly ground black pepper

Method:
1. Cook pasta according to packet instructions.
2. Melt butter in a pan and gently fry garlic and ginger until soft (about 5 minutes).
3. Stir in milk, lemon rind and juice and coriander, then toss in prawns.
4. Drain pasta and toss with prawn mixture and avocado.
5. Season and serve with salad and crusty bread.

HAGGIS CANNELLONI

(Serves 4)

Absolutely delicious! My family thinks this is even better than lasagne, but we are great haggis lovers. You can adjust quantities easily to make for large numbers. Serve with salad, crusty bread and red wine.

Ingredients:
1 x 450g haggis
250g pkt fresh lasagne sheets
400g tin chopped tomatoes
1 tbsp olive oil
1 onion, chopped
1 pepper, chopped
40g/1½oz butter
40g/1½oz plain flour
500ml/18fl oz milk
110g/4oz cheddar cheese, grated

Method:
1. Preheat the oven to 180°C, Gas Mark 4.
2. Fry the pepper and onion until soft, stir in the tomatoes. Pour into an ovenproof dish.
3. Take the haggis out of its packaging and break up into a bowl.
4. Cut the lasagne sheets in half and put haggis onto the lasagne sheet. Roll up into a cannelloni tube shape and put on top of the tomato mix. Continue till all haggis and sheets have been used up.
5. To make the white sauce, melt the butter add the flour and cook for 1 minute. Slowly add milk and keep stirring into a sauce.
6. Pour the sauce over the tubes and sprinkle with grated cheese.
7. Put in oven for 50 minutes.

IAIN'S SPAGHETTI CARBONARA

(Serves 2)

My husband Iain has his own way of changing dishes to suit his tastes and often they are a great success. This is one of them. He usually makes it on a Wednesday after I have finished my night shifts, served with a glass of red wine, garlic bread and a candle of course. What a treat!

Ingredients:
a little olive oil
2 eggs, whisked in a bowl
enough spaghetti for two people
1 onion, finely diced
½ pkt of bacon lardons or 4 slices of whatever bacon you have in the fridge, chopped or cut small with scissors
300ml/½ pint whipping cream
2 tbsp fresh parmesan cheese, grated - I have found fresh parmesan is much better although expensive, the taste is well worth it

Method:

1. Sauté diced bacon and onion in olive oil until soft. Leave to one side.
2. Meanwhile cook spaghetti according to instructions until *al dente* (just cooked with a bite). Drain and put back into the hot pan.
3. Add beaten eggs to hot spaghetti and stir until eggs are cooked and stuck to spaghetti.
4. Now add the cream, parmesan cheese, bacon and onion. Stir on low heat until warmed through.
5. Serve on warm plates with extra parmesan grated over the top.

SALMON AND ASPARAGUS LASAGNE

(Serves 6-8)

If you want to freeze this, do so before stage 7 and thaw overnight before baking.

Ingredients:

85g/3oz butter
85g/3oz plain flour
1.4 litres/2½ pints milk
142ml carton single cream
½ tsp nutmeg
2 garlic cloves, crushed
3 tbsp fresh dill, chopped
6 tbsp fresh chives, snipped
100g/3½oz parmesan, freshly grated
350g/12oz dried lasagne sheets
900g/2lb skinless salmon fillet, cut into large chunks
250g/9oz thin asparagus, cut into 5cm/2" lengths

Method:

1. Preheat oven to 200°C, Gas Mark 6.
2. Heat the butter in a pan, add and cook the flour for 1 minute. Gradually whisk in the milk, then the cream. Add half the nutmeg and the garlic. Cook, stirring till thickened and smooth. Simmer 2 minutes.
3. Remove from heat and stir in dill, half the chives and most of the parmesan (saving some for the top). Check seasoning and add more nutmeg if needed.
4. Spread a little sauce over the base of a 37cm x 25cm x 6cm/15" x 10" x 2 ½" ovenproof dish. Arrange a layer of lasagne sheets, overlapping, on top. Follow with a third of the salmon and asparagus, followed by some sauce.
5. Continue to layer up the lasagne finishing with a layer of pasta topped with sauce.
6. Sprinkle with the rest of the chives and parmesan.
7. Bake for 45 minutes until cooked through (check pasta is cooked) and golden on top.

VEGETABLE LASAGNE
(Serves 6)
Recommended by Barbara who saw it in a magazine a few years ago. Freezes well.

Ingredients:
4 tbsp olive oil
1 large aubergine or 2 large courgettes, cut into cubes
350g/12oz mushrooms, chopped
4 roasted red peppers, chopped – or use a jar
700g jar passata with onions and garlic
8-10 fresh lasagne sheets
200g/8oz frozen spinach, defrosted
250g/9oz ricotta cheese
25g/1oz parmesan cheese, grated
25g/1oz pine nuts

Method:
1. Preheat oven to 180ºC, Gas Mark 4.
2. Heat 2 tbsp oil in a large frying pan. Fry the aubergines or courgettes for 5 minutes then tip in a bowl. Fry the mushrooms in remaining oil then mix with the aubergines or courgettes, and red pepper.
3. Spoon ½ the vegetables into a 20cm x 30cm/8" x 12" baking dish, next spoon ½ the passata over and then top with a layer of lasagne sheets.
4. Repeat the layers with the rest of the vegetable mixture, the passata and a layer of lasagne sheets.
5. Drain excess liquid from the spinach and mix together with the ricotta and ½ of the parmesan. Spoon over the lasagne and sprinkle with the remaining parmesan and pine nuts.
6. Cover with tin foil and bake for 20 minutes, uncover, then bake for a further 10 minutes until brown and serve with a green salad.

PAGLIA E FIENO (pea and bacon)
(Serves 4)
Delicious and easy.

Ingredients:
55g/2oz butter
225g/8oz fresh garden peas
225g/8oz pancetta (or bacon, chopped)
150ml/¼ pint double cream
225g/8oz (or less) parmesan cheese, freshly grated
225g/8oz pasta (any sort)

Method:
1. Sauté pancetta (or bacon), pour off any fat.
2. Add butter and melt, then add peas and sauté lightly.
3. Add the cream and reduce slightly.
4. Cook the pasta in salted boiling water until *al dente*.
5. Add the cooked, drained pasta to the cream mixture, sprinkle with parmesan and toss lightly.
6. Serve immediately

Main Meals

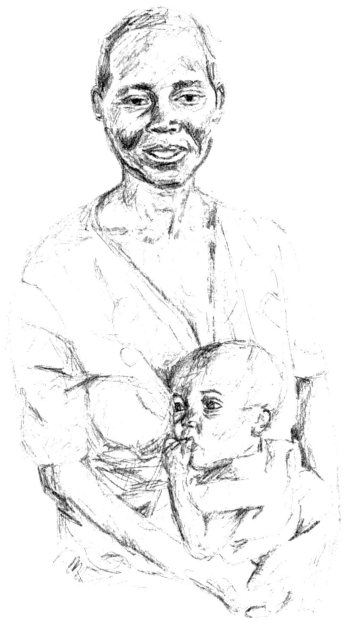

ALL IN ONE CHICKEN AND LEEK BAKE

(Serves 4)

I had this for supper at my dear friend Maureen's house. Her Mum Elsie makes it regularly for her as it can be made and cooked a day or so before needed, portioned, kept in the fridge, and heated in the microwave. When it goes cold the starch in the potatoes helps keep the ingredients together so it is very easy to cut. Apart from all this it tastes wonderful.

Ingredients:
a little olive oil and a knob of butter
3 chicken breasts, diced
4 leeks, sliced
about 3-4 potatoes depending on size, peeled
300ml/½ pint double cream
1 tsp grain mustard
grated cheddar cheese for the top

Method:
1. Preheat oven to 180°C, Gas Mark 4.
2. Sauté leeks in oil and butter until soft, lay on the bottom of a lasagne type dish.
3. Cook diced chicken and put in dish on top of leeks.
4. Parboil potatoes and slice fairly thickly. Then layer on top of chicken, overlapping slightly.
5. Mix mustard with cream and pour over the ingredients.
6. Cover with grated cheese.
7. Cook for approx 30 minutes.

AMERICAN CHICKEN

(Serves 4)

A popular tea with the teenagers. Serve with potato wedges (see p51 Book Two), sour cream dip and salad.

Ingredients:
4 chicken breasts
4 thick slices cheddar cheese
4 rashers back bacon
2 tbsp Hoi Sin sauce
1 can Diet Coke
1 heaped tsp cornflour, mixed in 2 tbsp cold milk till smooth

Method:
1. Preheat oven to 180°C, Gas Mark 4.
2. Make a pocket down the middle of each chicken breast and stuff with the cheese.
3. Wrap each breast with a bacon rasher and place in an ovenproof dish.
4. Spread Hoi Sin sauce over chicken parcels and pour Coke over.
5. Cook for approx 35 minutes.
6. Drain cooking liquid into a small pan and bring to boil, whisk in cornflour mixture, simmer gently till gravy thickens. Add more Coke if too thick, season to taste and pour back over chicken.
7. Serve.

EL VINO PAELLA ON THE BBQ

(Serves 6 as a main meal)

This recipe has stood the test of four Scottish summer barbeques…they come back for more every time. If it rains then plan B is to cook it on the oven top…placed over two rings and turned frequently so it heats evenly. - *Neil Watt*

Ingredients:

2 red onions, roughly chopped
3 garlic cloves, finely chopped
450g/1lb boneless, skinless chicken thighs (cut into chunks, don't remove excess fat)
450g/1lb ripe tomatoes, chopped
1 red pepper, chopped
225g/8oz fine green beans, trimmed and cut in half
110g/4oz frozen peas
good pinch saffron threads
2 litres/3½ pints vegetable or chicken stock (plus a dash of white wine)
4 tbsp olive oil
100g/3½oz chorizo sausage, sliced thinly
2 tsp paprika
450g/1lb arbrorio rice
about 10 large raw prawns in shells (langoustines are best and most decorative)
about 12 mussels
large handful parsley, chopped roughly

To serve:
good sized lemon wedges

Method:

1. Set up the barbeque making sure the paella pan is level. Light the barbeque and when ready spread out the coals evenly. Let it cool a little before starting cooking.
2. Separately heat the stock and add the saffron threads, bring it to a simmer.
3. Using the paella pan on the barbeque heat half the oil.
4. Add the chorizo, fry quickly, turning until crisp at the edges, then set aside.
5. Add the remaining oil to the pan, then add the chicken and fry quickly, stirring, until lightly coloured. Stir in the onion and garlic and fry, stirring till onion is going soft.
6. Stir in the tomatoes and pepper. Season, then add the beans and paprika and stir well. Sprinkle in the rice, stirring until the grains begin to soak up the oil. Stir gently to avoid making the rice go too sticky.
7. Add a cup full of hot stock. When it starts to bubble and soak into the rice, add more, stirring well (but gently). Continue adding stock and stirring until the rice is just tender – this should take about 10-15 minutes. Return the chorizo to the pan and add the prawns and mussels. If you've got langoustines lay them with tails at the centre of the pan.
8. Cook for 2-3 minutes, until the prawns/langoustines turn pink and the mussels open. Season to taste.
9. Remove the paella from the heat and cover the pan with foil. Leave for 5 minutes to cool slightly then sprinkle the parsley over. Serve with lemon wedges.

CHAIRMAN'S CHICKEN

(Serves 8-10)

It is one of my Mum's favourites for family dinners. It is easy to cook, very tasty and always seems to contribute to a great atmosphere around the table. – *Jack McConnell*

Ingredients:

1.4kg/3lb cooked chicken
450g/1lb partly cooked broccoli
2 tins Campbell's Cream of Chicken soup
3 tbsp Hellman's mayonnaise
4 tbsp lemon juice
2 cups grated cheese
2 cups breadcrumbs

Method:

1. Preheat oven to 180°C, Gas Mark 4.
2. Lay the chicken and broccoli in a casserole dish and mix in the soup, mayonnaise and lemon juice.
3. Spread the cheese and breadcrumbs over the top, cover and cook in a moderate oven for approx 1 hour.
4. Serve with potatoes and salad.

CHICKEN CACCIATORE

(Serves 6)

Cameron fell in love with this dish when it was first cooked for him by his Godfather Alistair Moffat. On one of our family and friends Easter holidays to Arran, he and his pals aged 14 chose to cook it for 16 of us for dinner. A great success. - *The Pow Family*

Ingredients:

2kg/4lb 8oz chicken, or 4 large chicken portions
3 tbsp olive oil
2 large onions, peeled and sliced
2 garlic cloves, peeled and crushed
400g tin tomatoes
2 tbsp fresh parsley, chopped - or 1 tbsp dried parsley
2 tbsp fresh basil, finely chopped - or 1 tbsp dried basil
1 tbsp tomato purée
150ml/¼ pint red wine
salt and lots of freshly ground black pepper
optional - we add black pitted olives and a large handful of roughly chopped mushrooms half way through the cooking.

To serve:
fresh basil leaves

Method:

1. Preheat oven to 160°C, Gas Mark 3.
2. Cut the chicken into roughly eight pieces and remove skin.
3. Heat oil in pan and fry the chicken pieces until browned all over. Transfer to large casserole or roasting dish.

4. Add onions and garlic to the pan and fry until golden brown. Add the tomatoes with their juice, the parsley, the chopped basil, tomato purée and wine. Then bring to the boil. Add salt and pepper.
5. Pour over the chicken, cover the casserole with lid or tinfoil and cook in a preheated oven for about 1 hour or until tender.
6. Sprinkle with torn fresh basil and serve with chunks of crusty bread and salad or with new potatoes - and a glass of red wine.

CHICKEN AND MANGO CURRY
(Serves 4)
A fruity curry dish – sweet and creamy but with a spicy kick. Spiciness can be altered by the number of red chillies used. I recommend medium red chilli peppers, de-seeded, but any can be used, with or without seeds. The recipe includes Panch Phoran (an Indian 5-spice mixture) and Garam Masala, both available from some supermarkets or Indian grocers. - *Mike Watt*

Ingredients:
4 boneless skinless chicken breasts, chopped into 2.5cm/1" pieces
2 mangos, peeled and chopped
2 medium onions, finely chopped
4 garlic cloves, chopped
2-4 medium red chilli peppers (depending on heat required), de-seeded and chopped
5cm/2" chunk of ginger root, skinned and chopped
100g/3½oz golden sultanas
60g/2¼oz unsalted butter or ghee (Indian purified butter)
1 tbsp white wine vinegar
1½ cups water
2 tbsp Panch Phoran (Indian Five Spice)
2 tbsp Garam Masala
2 tsp mild yellow curry powder
1 cup double cream
coriander to garnish
salt and pepper

Method:
1. In a large skillet or saucepan melt butter over medium heat.
2. Add Panch Phoran, Garam Masala and gently fry for 1 minute. (Careful not to burn spice mix). Add ginger and garlic and chilli - fry briefly, coating all with butter and spice mix. (Free with a little water if the mix becomes too dry)
3. Add onion, vinegar and water, stir thoroughly and bring to the boil. Add ½ the mangos and simmer for 3-4 minutes.
4. Remove from heat and transfer to blender – purée until smooth. Add salt and pepper.
5. Return mixture to pan and add chicken pieces. Add curry powder. Bring back to boil and simmer for further 10 minutes to cook chicken. (Check chicken is cooked through with a sharp knife).
6. Add remainder of mango (keep a few small chunks for garnish) and sultanas and heat through, reducing heat to very low simmer for another 5 minutes. Add cream and stir through.
7. Garnish with small pieces of mango and a few coriander leaves. Serve with boiled or fried rice.

CHICKEN COATED IN TARRAGON WITH LEMON POTATOES

(Serves 4)

This is a low fat delicious meal. We had this at our friends May and Raymond's, house who were following a very healthy diet but still enjoyed entertaining. The potatoes won it for me.

Ingredients:

new potatoes, enough for four people
450ml/¾ pint chicken stock made with a stock cube
juice and zest of a lemon
4 chicken breasts
a little olive oil
4 tbsp fresh tarragon or if you can't get fresh use about 2 tbsp of dried tarragon, fresh coriander is a good alternative.
4 tbsp fresh parsley, chopped in a mug with scissors
cherry tomatoes on the vine, cut into four
a little granulated sugar

Method:

1. Preheat oven to 200ºC, Gas Mark 6.
2. Place washed potatoes in a saucepan with the stock, 2 tbsp of lemon juice and 1 tsp of lemon zest. Bring to the boil and simmer, covered, for about 15 minutes until tender.
3. Meanwhile mix the herbs, except 1 tbsp of parsley, with remaining lemon zest together on a plate. Coat the chicken breasts in the olive oil with your hands and roll the chicken in the herb mixture to cover. Place in a lightly greased roasting tin.
4. Drizzle the remaining lemon juice over the chicken and cook in oven for 10 minutes.
5. Add the tomatoes to the chicken, sprinkle with the sugar and place back in the oven for a further 10 minutes or until the juices from the chicken run clear and they are cooked.
6. When the potatoes are tender, remove the lid, increase the heat and boil until the liquid has reduced. You should have a syrupy mixture left. Toss the potatoes in the juices with the remaining tbsp of parsley.
7. Serve the chicken on a hot plate with the lemony potatoes, tomatoes and a green vegetable if you wish.

CHICKEN WITH LEEKS AND TARRAGON

(Serves 4)

This chicken dish I had at my friend Susan's house in Dunblane. She always seems to come up with great dishes that I copy. Her grandparents were Irish and I think she got this dish from an Irish cookbook. I love it and it has always gone down well when I've cooked it for friends. The flavours all work so well together. Serve with boiled rice or new potatoes and green vegetables. - *Judith Gibson*

Ingredients:

4 chicken fillets
4-6 rashers bacon – chopped
4 thin leeks, chopped
Knorr concentrated chicken stock/bouillon (approx 250ml/9fl oz)
300ml/½ pint crème fraîche
boiled water
4 stalks fresh tarragon

Method:

1. Preheat oven to 180°C, Gas Mark 4.
2. Brown the chicken fillets and put in casserole dish in oven.
3. Fry chopped bacon for 5 minutes and add to chicken.
4. Fry leeks, add crème fraîche and bouillon. Stir in water to desired consistency.
5. Simmer.
6. Place tarragon over the chicken and add sauce.
7. Cook for 30-40 minutes.

CHICKEN ZORBA

(Serves 4)

This is an old recipe of Jane's, which she recommended we share. It is easy and tasty.

Ingredients:

4 chicken breasts
150g tub Greek yoghurt
170g tub houmous
2 tbsp olive oil
juice of 2 limes
1 level tsp coriander
1 level tsp cumin
½ tsp turmeric
pinch salt
1 tbsp freshly chopped mint

To serve:
4 pitta breads
mixed salad leaves
tomatoes, sliced
yellow pepper, chopped

Method:

1. To make marinade blend together lime juice, spices, salt and mint.
2. Cut chicken into thin strips, add to marinade, leave in fridge for 1 hour.
3. Mix yoghurt and houmous.
4. Heat oil and cook chicken for 8–10 minutes.
5. Toast pitta breads and cut in half. Open and spread with houmous and yoghurt.
6. Fill with chicken and salad.

CHRISTMAS PIE

(Serves 10-12 slices)

Given to me by Caroline last Christmas. I made this in June using dried cranberries and cashew nuts as I couldn't get chestnuts. It worked beautifully and looked very impressive. Great for a cold buffet – especially on Boxing Day as you could make it a couple of days before. Can be frozen.

Ingredients:
2 tbsp olive oil
knob butter
1 onion, finely chopped
500g/1lb 2oz sausagemeat or skinned sausages
grated zest of 1 lemon
100g/3½oz fresh white breadcrumbs
85g/ 3oz ready-to-eat dried apricots, chopped
50g/1¾oz chestnuts, canned or vacuum packed, chopped
2 tsp chopped fresh or 1 tsp dried thyme
100g/3½oz cranberries, fresh or frozen
500g/1lb 2oz boneless, skinless chicken breasts
500g pkt ready-made shortcrust pastry
beaten egg, to glaze

Method:
1. Preheat oven to 190ºC, Gas Mark 5.
2. Heat 1 tbsp oil and the butter in a frying pan, then add the onion and fry for 5 minutes until softened. Cool slightly. Tip the sausagemeat, lemon zest, breadcrumbs, apricots, chestnuts, thyme, the onion and cranberries into a bowl. Mix everything together with your hands, adding plenty of pepper and a little salt.
3. Cut each chicken breast into three fillets lengthwise and season all over with salt and pepper. Heat the remaining oil in the frying pan and fry the chicken fillets quickly until browned, about 6-8 minutes.
4. Roll out ⅔ of the pastry to line a 21cm/8" springform or deep loose-based tart tin. Press in half the sausage mix and spread to level. Then add the chicken pieces in one layer and cover with the rest of the sausage mix. Press down lightly.
5. Roll out the remaining pastry to form a lid. Brush the edges of the pie with beaten egg and cover with the pastry lid. Pinch the edges to seal, then trim. Brush the top of the pie with egg then roll out the trimmings to make holly leaf shapes and berries. Decorate the pie and brush again with egg.
6. Set the tin on a baking sheet and bake for 50-60 minutes then cool in the tin for 15 minutes. Remove and leave to cool completely.

HONEY GLAZED CHICKEN

(Serves 3)

Recipe given to me by my neighbour Jackie and it is delicious. I used chicken breasts as she suggests and cut them in the side half way to flatten out.

Ingredients:
2 frying chickens (Poussins)
2 tbsp oil
2 tbsp clear honey
1 tbsp Dijon mustard
2 tsp curry powder
½ tsp salt

Method:

1. Preheat oven to 225°C, Gas Mark 7½.
2. Halve the chickens (you can use chicken breasts with the skin on instead)
3. Brush a casserole dish with oil and lay cut side of chicken down on base.
4. Mix honey with mustard, curry powder and salt then brush over chicken.
5. Cover casserole with foil loosely and seal.
6. Cook in the centre of the oven for 30 minutes.
7. Remove foil and cook for a further 20 minutes until skin is crisp and brown.
   I serve with roast potatoes cooked at the same time and steamed baby vegetables.

COD ON BEAN RAGOÛT

(Serves 6)

The bean ragoût makes a change from the usual potatoes and vegetables. Handy for dinner parties as you can prepare the ragoût ahead of time. - *Karen Matthews*

Ingredients:

6 cod fillets
1 chorizo sausage, skinned and chopped
1 onion, chopped
1 tsp fresh rosemary, finely chopped
1 garlic clove, crushed
1 tsp tomato purée
small glass white wine
pinch sugar
1 tbsp red wine vinegar
400g tin chopped tomatoes
2 x 400g tins beans, drained (butter, cannellini, barlotti etc) according to taste
450ml/ ¾ pint vegetable or light chicken stock
small handful fresh parsley, chopped
1 tbsp olive oil
salt and pepper

Method:

1. Preheat oven to 200ºC, Gas Mark 6,
2. Fry the chorizo for 2 minutes in a dry frying pan and remove, leaving the oil in the pan.
3. Add the onion, garlic and rosemary to pan and fry gently for 3-4 minutes.
4. Pour in the wine and turn the heat up until the wine has reduced by half.
5. Add vinegar and sugar and allow to bubble for a minute. Stir in the tomato purée and cook for another minute.
6. Add the tomatoes, chorizo and ½ pint of stock and simmer for 15-20 minutes then put in the beans and let them warm through. If it's too thick add more stock.
7. Add parsley and season to taste. Keep warm.
8. Heat olive oil in frying pan until fairly hot, season the cod with salt and pepper and seal each piece in the pan for a minute on each side.
9. Place in oven at 200ºC, Gas Mark 6, for 5-7 minutes, depending on thickness, until cooked through.
10. Serve a piece of cod on top of the ragoût.

EASY PEASY RISOTTO

(Serves 4)

This is a multi tasking, working mum's tea! Put it in the oven and get on with all the other jobs you need to do. – *Gail McLaren*

Ingredients:
1 tbsp oil
1 onion, chopped
300g/10½oz risotto rice
100ml/3½fl oz white wine
400g tin chopped tomatoes
200g/7oz frozen Mediterranean chargrilled vegetables
500ml/18fl oz vegetable stock
a handful flat-leaf parsley, chopped

To serve:
parmesan shavings

Method:
1. Preheat oven to 200°C, Gas Mark 6.
2. Fry the onion in the oil for a few minutes until soft.
3. Turn up the heat, add the rice, stir and fry for a minute.
4. Pour in the wine and stir until absorbed then add the tomatoes and frozen vegetables and 400ml/16fl oz of the stock.
5. Cover and bake in the oven for 25 minutes until the rice is tender and creamy.
6. Stir in the remaining stock and parsley, season and scatter with parmesan. Serve.

IRISH STEW

(Serves 4-6)

Of course an Irish colleen has an Irish Stew recipe! This one has memories of Loch Tay during the October holidays when the girls were small. We would come back to the cottage with the aroma of the stew to welcome us. This is a made up version and quantities can be adjusted to suit.

Ingredients:
about 2 tbsp olive or sunflower oil
450-900g/1-2lb neck of lamb, or shoulder of lamb
2 carrots, peeled and sliced
2 onions, sliced
about 900g/2lbs of potatoes, peeled and sliced – more or less according to number of people
about 300ml/½ pint stock, made with a lamb stock cube
some plain flour with a pinch of mixed herbs added
salt and pepper

Method:
1. Preheat oven to 150-160ºC, Gas Mark 2-3.
2. Prepare lamb by cutting into chunks keeping most of the fat on the meat. Discard any big pieces of fat. Toss all the meat in the flour to coat.
3. Heat the oil in a large casserole dish that you can put into the oven and brown the meat in batches. Leave the meat on one side.
4. Soften the onion in the remaining oil adding the carrots and potatoes. Stir altogether.
5. Put meat back in pot with juices and enough stock to just cover all the ingredients. Add salt and pepper to taste.
6. Cook for about 2 hours, stir occasionally. This can also be cooked in a slow cooker.

JANE'S CHICKEN AND COUSCOUS SALAD

(Serves 4)

I found this on an old calendar, it's very easy, very tasty and I use it again and again. – *Jane Arnot*

Ingredients:
4 chicken breasts, cut into bite sized pieces
2 tbsp mango chutney
2 tbsp mild curry paste
1 tsp turmeric
50ml/2fl oz olive oil
1 tbsp white wine vinegar
200g/7oz couscous, cooked in 250ml boiling water as per instructions
200g/7oz cherry tomatoes, halved
4 tbsp fresh mint, chopped

Method:
1. Mix the chutney and spices with 25ml/1fl oz of the oil.
2. Add the chicken to this mixture and toss well.
3. Cover and leave to marinade for a couple of hours or overnight.
4. Cook the chicken, either in a hot oven for 15-20 minutes till cooked or fry in a pan if preferred.
5. Mix in the remaining oil and vinegar and cool. Drain off any liquids.
6. Stir into the couscous with the tomatoes and mint.

LAMB FILLET WITH REDCURRANT SAUCE

(Serves 3)

I had this at Debbie's house. I adore roast leg of lamb as I am sure many of you do and this sauce is just perfect to make the dish dinner party material. Double up on ingredients if you are using a leg of lamb. Spoon half the cream mixture over the lamb 30 minutes before the end of cooking. Mix the red wine and redcurrant jelly with the remaining cream mixture to make your gravy. Lovely with the Parsnip Bake (in Accompaniments chapter), roast potatoes and carrots.

Ingredients:
150ml/5fl oz soured cream
1 garlic clove, crushed
1 tsp wholegrain mustard
salt and pepper
450g/1lb lamb fillet
2 tbsp dry red wine
1 tbsp redcurrant jelly

Method:
1. Preheat oven to 180°C, Gas Mark 4.
2. Mix ⅓ of soured cream with garlic and mustard. Season.
3. Put lamb in roasting tin and spoon mixture over.
4. Roast for 30 minutes then transfer to serving dish.
5. Add wine to the roasting tin and stir in redcurrant jelly.
6. Bring to the boil then add remainder of soured cream and boil for 2-3 minutes until thickened slightly.
7. Thinly slice lamb and serve with sauce spooned over.

LAYERED SAUSAGE HOTPOT

(Serves 4)
This is a great midweek family meal and cheap.

Ingredients:
6 back bacon rashers
6 pork sausages, skinned
1 onion, chopped
400g tin baked beans
400g tin chopped tomatoes
5 medium potatoes, peeled and thinly sliced
50g/1¾oz cheese, grated

Method:
1. Preheat oven to 200°C, Gas Mark 6.
2. Cut the rind from the bacon, slice the sausages in half lengthways, and flatten out.
3. Using a large, deep ovenproof dish, begin to layer the ingredients.
4. Begin with a layer of potato, and then add tomatoes, beans, onion, bacon and sausages.
5. Continue layering all of the ingredients, and finally top with potato slices.
6. Cover the dish with tin foil and bake for approximately 1½ hours.
7. Remove the foil and add the grated cheese.
8. Return to the oven for a further 20 minutes until golden brown.

MARINADED BEEF OR VENISON CASSEROLE

(Serves 4)
I love the marinade in this recipe and each of the other recipe books has a hearty, all in one family casserole recipe.

Ingredients:

1kg/2lb 4oz beef or venison, cubed
50g/1¾oz butter
salt and pepper
1 tbsp fresh rosemary, chopped
4 medium carrots, peeled and quartered
8 small onions, peeled
8 mushrooms
400g tin tomatoes
3 medium potatoes, peeled and halved
3 tbsp tomato purée

For the marinade:
350ml/12fl oz red wine
250ml/9fl oz beef stock
3 tbsp olive oil
1 large onion, thinly sliced
8 black peppercorns
2 tbsp fresh parsley, chopped
1 tbsp fresh rosemary, chopped
bouquet garni
3 garlic cloves, crushed

Method:
1. Mix together all of the marinade ingredients in a shallow dish.
2. Add the beef or venison and leave in the fridge for at least 12 hours or overnight.
3. Remove the meat from the marinade and pat dry using kitchen towel.
4. Reserve the rest of the marinade - discarding the peppercorns and the bouquet garni.
5. Melt the butter in a flameproof casserole dish and add the beef or venison cubes to brown.
6. Stir in the remaining marinade and rosemary and season to taste.
7. Bring to the boil, cover and simmer on a low heat for 1 hour (beef) or 1 ½ hours (venison). Alternatively cook in a low oven for the same time.
8. Add the carrots, onions, potatoes, mushrooms and tomato purée and stir well.
9. Cover and simmer for a further 1 hour or place back in oven until meat is tender and vegetables are cooked.

SWEETLY SPICED LAMB WITH DATES

(Serves 4)

I like to make ahead, cool quickly and reheat when required adding more water if necessary.

Ingredients:
1 tbsp olive oil
2 onions, chopped
500g/1lb 2oz boneless lean lamb (leg), diced
500g/1lb 2oz sweet potatoes, cut into small chunks
1 tsp ground coriander
1 tsp cinnamon
2 tbsp tomato purée
110g/4oz soft pitted dates
2 tbsp fresh coriander, chopped
600ml/1 pint boiling water

Method:
1. Heat the oil in a large pan and add the onion and lamb and quickly fry until the lamb is lightly browned.
2. Add the sweet potatoes and spices, mix well.
3. Pour in 600ml/1 pint boiling water and the tomato purée. Bring to the boil.
4. Cover and simmer for 15 minutes, add the dates and cook a further 10 minutes, until sweet potatoes and lamb are tender.
5. Sprinkle with coriander and serve with couscous.

QUORN AND MANGO CURRY

(Serves 2-3)

My friend Mags made this for a girls night earlier in the year and it was so yum that I had to ask her for the recipe! You can also add other chopped vegetables and/or beans to bulk it out. – *Heather Sutherland*

Ingredients:

1 pkt quorn chicken pieces or 2 large chicken breasts
1 large onion, chopped
sunflower oil
110g/4oz mushrooms, sliced
1 green or red pepper, cut into strips
½ a 530g jar of mango chutney (chunky if you can get it)
900ml/1½ pints chicken or vegetable stock if using quorn **or**
450ml/16fl oz chicken stock if using chicken breasts
cream, to taste

Curry spices:
2 tsp cumin
1 tsp coriander
1 tsp turmeric
1 tsp ground ginger (or 1 tbsp fresh ginger, finely chopped)
1 bird's eye chilli (optional)
pinch salt and pepper

Method:

1. Pour a little sunflower oil into a wok or large frying pan and when hot add quorn (or chicken) and vegetables and stir fry for 5 – 10 minutes.
2. Add stock, mango chutney and curry spices and stir well.
3. Cover and simmer for 30 minutes, stirring occasionally.
4. Towards the end of cooking time add cream to your taste and simmer for 5 minutes.

ROASTED SEA BASS ON A BED OF SWEET POTATO GRATIN WITH A LEMON THYME BUTTER FONDUE

(Serves 4)

It looks long and complicated but it is not. Read through the recipe first and you will see. The simplicity of the fish lying on the yummy potatoes is overall very easy, yet looks so professional. This is dinner party material. The sweet potato gratin is best made a day in advance. - *The Bluebell Inn, Emsworth.*

Ingredients:

8 x 200g/7oz sea bass fillets (ask the fishmonger to scale, fillet and pin bone)
seasoned flour

For sweet potato gratin:
1kg/2lb 4oz sweet potatoes, peeled and thinly sliced
500ml/18fl oz double cream
2 tsp nutmeg, freshly ground
1 garlic clove, crushed
200g/7oz grated gruyère cheese
salt and pepper

For the sauce:
2 shallots, finely chopped
500ml/18fl oz fish stock (fresh if possible)
125ml/4fl oz double cream
100g/3½ oz unsalted butter, cold
juice of ½ lemon
25g/1oz fresh lemon thyme
stalks of the lemon thyme

To serve:
chives, snipped

Method:

For sweet potato gratin:
1. Preheat oven to 200°C, Gas Mark 6.
2. In a large saucepan put the potatoes, cream, garlic, nutmeg and season to taste. Cook for approximately 10 minutes until potatoes are almost cooked.
3. Layer the potatoes in a greased gratin dish, season and add the cheese to each layer.
4. Pour the rest of the cream mixture over the potatoes and sprinkle the top with the remaining cheese.
5. Bake in the preheated oven until the cheese is golden brown.
6. If baked in advance, leave to cool, cover and press with a tray and weights. Refrigerate.
7. To reheat, place in hot oven for 10-15 minutes.

For roasted sea bass:
1. Preheat oven to 180°C, Gas Mark 4.
2. Score the fish on the skin side with a sharp knife.
3. Pass through seasoned flour, and shake off any excess flour.
4. Place the fish skin side down in a pan of smoking hot olive oil and turn the fish when the skin is golden brown.
5. Transfer to a baking tray and cook in a preheated oven for 5-10 minutes depending on the thickness of the fillets.
6. While the fish is cooking make the sauce.

For the sauce:
1. Sweat the shallots in a saucepan, retaining a clear colour.
2. Add the fish stock and thyme stalks and reduce the mixture to a glacé.
3. Add the double cream and reduce slightly.
4. Add the diced cold butter and swirl the pan, keeping it in motion until the butter is melted (this process is called monte au beurre, and will help thicken and emulsify the sauce).
5. Remove the lemon thyme stalks.
6. Add the lemon juice and thyme and season to taste.

To serve:
Slice the potato gratin into portions, and place in centre of hot plate. Put the sea bass fillets on top of the potato. Pour the sauce around the potato and garnish with fresh chives.

ROASTED COD WITH CHEESE AND ONION MASH AND CHIMICHURRI

(Serves 4)

Another wonderful fish dish served on cheesy potatoes. Read through the recipe, don't be put off with the length of method and ingredients. It is very easy and you will be complimented greatly on the whole composition. Again dinner party material.
- *The Hermitage Restaurant, Emsworth.*

Ingredients:

4 x 200g/7oz fresh cod steaks (thick with skins on)
4 large maris piper potatoes, peeled and cut
1 bunch spring onions, cut into small rings
¾ cup virgin olive oil
2 lemons, juiced
90g/3¼oz mature cheddar cheese, grated
2 small shallots
50ml/2fl oz cream (double or single)
⅓ cup curly parsley, chopped
1 tsp oregano, chopped
1 clove garlic, crushed
125g/4½oz butter

Method:

For the Chimichurri sauce:

Can be made the day before but remove from fridge 2 hours before using to allow flavours to come through **or** make at least a couple of hours before using to allow flavours to infuse.

1. Put 2 tbsp lemon juice into a bowl and add ½ cup olive oil, chopped shallots, basil, oregano, parsley and crushed garlic with a pinch of salt and pepper and stir.
2. Place in fridge to infuse.

For the cod and mash:

1. Preheat oven to 200°C, Gas Mark 6.
2. Cook potatoes in boiling salted water.
3. In a sauté pan, heat ¼ cup olive oil and a knob of butter until it bubbles.
4. Place the cod steaks in the pan with the skin sides down, and cook on a moderate heat for 5-6 minutes until the skin turns golden brown in colour.
5. Turn the cod and cook the other side for 2 minutes.
6. Remove the cod and place onto a baking tray and season.
7. Place in the centre of oven and cook for 6-10 minutes (will depend on thickness of fish).
8. While the fish is in the oven, drain the cooked potatoes and allow them to air dry for a few minutes.
9. Place potatoes in a bowl and mash with butter, cream, grated cheese, salt, pepper and spring onions.

To serve:

Place the mash on hot plates. Briefly place each piece of cooked cod onto kitchen towel to absorb any grease, then position on the potato. Spoon the chimichurri sauce over top. Serve with a green salad on the side.

SLOW COOKED SALMON WITH LENTILS

(Serves 4)

An unusual combination of ingredients creating wonderful flavours. Don't be put off by the amount of chopping – you can prepare the lentils in advance and reheat when required (stage 5). - *Margie Aikman*

Ingredients:

For the herb butter:
2 tbsp unsalted butter at room temperature
1 small shallot, finely minced
2 tsp fresh flat leaf parsley, minced
1½ tsp Dijon mustard
sea salt and freshly ground pepper

For the lentils:
3½ tbsp unsalted butter
½ large onion, minced
½ large carrot, peeled & diced
1 small inner celery stalk, diced
2 cloves garlic, minced
750ml/27fl oz chicken stock
1 large fresh thyme sprig
220g/7oz French green lentils
sea salt and freshly ground pepper
1½ tbsp minced fresh flat leaf parsley

4 salmon fillets, skin removed
sea salt and freshly ground pepper

Method:
1. Preheat the oven to 150°C, Gas Mark 2.
2. Butter a baking dish large enough to hold the salmon in one layer.
3. Make the herb butter in a bowl by combining the butter, shallot, parsley & mustard. Mix until smooth. Season with salt & pepper.
4. Melt 2 tbsp butter in a large frying pan over a low heat. Add onion, carrot, celery & garlic and sauté until softened, about 20 minutes.
5. In a saucepan combine the stock & thyme and bring to a simmer. Add the lentils, cover partially, adjust heat to maintain a simmer, and cook until tender, 20-25 minutes. Remove from the heat and discard the thyme sprig. Using a slotted spoon add the lentils to the vegetables along with a few tbsp of their liquid. Season with salt & pepper, stir well then cover and simmer until the lentils have absorbed the liquid, about 10 minutes. Keep warm over a low heat. (You can prepare the lentils in advance and reheat at this stage).
6. Season the salmon fillets on both sides, place in the buttered baking dish and bake for 20-25 minutes until the fish just flakes.
7. Remove the lentils from the heat. Add the parsley and the remaining 1½ tbsp butter and stir until the butter melts. Divide the lentils among the warmed individual plates, place a salmon fillet on top and spread the top of each salmon fillet with the herb butter. Serve immediately.

ROSEMOUNT STREET'S SPECIAL FISH DISH

(Serves 6)

This is very easy to make and so delicious – even next day – if you have any left over!

- *Margaret Newlands*

Ingredients:
2 tbsp olive oil
1 large onion, chopped or sliced
2 red peppers, halved lengthwise, sliced thickly
1 large fennel bulb, roughly chopped
200g tin tomatoes
salt and pepper
2 tbsp capers, drained
small tsp sugar
6 cod fillets, skinned
1 jar tartar sauce
200g/7oz breadcrumbs – ciabatta crumbs are really good!
1 pinch paprika
3 tbsp parsley, chopped

Method:
1. Preheat oven to 200°C, Gas Mark 6.
2. Heat oil in a large frying pan and soften the onion.
3. Add the pepper, fennel and tomatoes and stir together, bring to the boil. Season.
4. Cook gently for 10 minutes, until fennel begins to soften.
5. Stir in the capers and sugar and transfer to flat ovenproof dish.
6. Season the fish on both sides and arrange over the vegetables.
7. Spread tartar sauce on each fillet and sprinkle with seasoned breadcrumbs and paprika.
8. Bake for 20 minutes till fish is cooked.
9. Sprinkle with chopped parsley and serve.

VEGETABLE TAGINE

(Serves 2)

To make this easier (for me!) I put all the spices together in an egg cup and then tip the lot in when required. I also made this for a friend who is allergic to onions and garlic by simply removing them and adjusting the spices. Still delicious! – *Heather Sutherland*

Ingredients:
1 small aubergine, roughly cut into 2.5cm/1" cubes
150g/5½oz butternut squash, peeled and roughly cut into 2.5cm/1" cubes
cooking spray
2 tsp olive oil
1 small onion, finely chopped
2 garlic cloves, finely chopped
1 small cinnamon stick
pinch of saffron
1 tsp runny honey
1 tsp ground coriander
1 tsp ground cumin
1 tsp paprika

400g tin chopped tomatoes
juice of 2 oranges
2 small courgettes, thickly sliced
5 dried apricots, roughly chopped
55g/2oz cooked chickpeas
25g/1oz whole almonds, toasted
1 tsp coriander, roughly chopped

Method:
1. Preheat oven to 180°C, Gas Mark 4.
2. Place the aubergine and butternut squash on a baking tray, spray lightly with cooking spray and roast in the oven for around 15 minutes or until tender.
3. Meanwhile, heat the olive oil in a medium saucepan and sweat the onion, garlic and cinnamon for 5 minutes.
4. Add the saffron, honey, coriander, cumin and paprika, and cook the spices for a minute.
5. Add the chopped tomatoes and fresh orange juice then bring the sauce to a boil.
6. Add the courgettes and apricots then lower the heat and simmer for 10 minutes.
7. Add the cooked aubergine and butternut squash to the sauce along with the chickpeas and cook for 5 minutes.
8. Serve the tagine with cooked couscous or brown rice and scatter the almonds and fresh coriander over the top.

POTATO, CHEESE & ONION PIE
(Serves 6)
My mother-in-law makes the most wonderful pastry and this is one of her traditional, comforting pies for all the family. – *Lorna Pascall*

Ingredient:
675g/1½lbs potatoes (after peeling), thinly sliced
2 tbsp olive oil
2 onions, thinly sliced
2 garlic cloves, chopped
5 tbsp double cream
55g/2oz sun-dried tomatoes in oil, drained and chopped
2 tbsp parsley, chopped
110g/4oz mature cheddar cheese, grated
salt and pepper
approx. 350– 450g/12–16oz shortcrust pastry

Method:
1. Preheat oven to 200°C, Gas Mark 6.
2. Cook potato slices in boiling water until soft – 7-10 minutes. Drain and dry.
3. Heat oil in large pan and cook onion and garlic, covered, until soft.
4. Add cream, sun-dried tomatoes and parsley. Season to taste and bring to boil stirring continuously until heated through. Leave to cool.
5. Roll out half the pastry and line a 20cm/8" diameter tin or dish.
6. Layer half the potatoes in the base of the pastry and pour over half the onion mixture and half the grated cheese.
7. Repeat these layers once more using all remaining ingredients.
8. Roll out remaining pastry and cover top of pie. Brush top with milk, make a hole in the centre and bake for 30 minutes.

DOREEN AND DAVY'S PIZZA

(Serves approx 2-4 people)

Doreen used to cook a few meals for us in Malawi. What a treat it was to come home after a long day to find a lovely homemade pizza ready waiting to go into the oven. Davy, her husband, works for Tarek as full time cook and this is his recipe. What I also liked about it was the two versions. If you don't have enough time the baking powder acts as a quick raising agent and the pizza tastes just as good.

Toppings for Pizza:
sun-dried tomato paste or tinned tomatoes or tomato purée
onions
peppers
chicken or tuna
any type of cheese
actually anything you want used up in the fridge

Pizza No 1 - using yeast

Ingredients:
2 cups bread flour
2 tsp dried yeast
½ cup warm water
1 tsp salt

Method No 1:
1. Mix all the ingredients with warm water to make a dough.
2. Knead the dough until it is soft.
3. Cover the dough with a damp tea towel for 2 hours.
4. Now knead again and roll out lightly on a floured surface.
5. Line baking tray and cover with pizza dough.
6. Spread tomato evenly, followed by chosen toppings.
7. Cook in preheated oven 190°C, Gas Mark 5 for about 15-20 minutes.

Pizza No 2 - using baking powder

Ingredients:
2 cups bread flour
2 tsp baking powder
1-2 cups cold water
1 tsp salt
¾-1 cup cooking oil

Method No 2:
1. Mix all the ingredients to make a dough.
2. Knead the dough until it is soft and let it stand for 30 minutes.
3. Roll out the dough on a floured surface.
4. Line baking tray and cover with pizza dough.
5. Spread tomato evenly, followed by chosen toppings.
6. Cook in preheated oven 190°C, Gas Mark 5 for about 15-20 minutes.

Delicious Desserts

BAKED ORANGE CHEESECAKE WITH CARAMELISED ORANGES

(Serves 10-12)

Just tastes like the real American cheesecake. The orange segments make all the difference. It is very rich so only serve a small piece to start. It is worth putting a small roasting tin half filled with boiling water on the shelf below your cheesecake whilst cooking as this will prevent the top from cracking.

Ingredients:

For the base:
150g/5½oz digestive biscuits, crushed to fine crumbs
75g/3¾oz unsalted butter, melted

For the filling:
50g/1¾oz unsalted butter, softened
150g/5½oz caster sugar
450g/1lb full-fat cream cheese
25g/1oz plain flour
zest of 2 oranges, finely grated
juice of 1 orange
3 eggs, separated
150ml/¼ pint whipping cream

For the caramelised oranges:
6 oranges
2 tbsp Grand Marnier or Cointreau
200g/7oz granulated sugar

Method:

1. Preheat oven to 170°C, Gas Mark 3.
2. Line a loose bottomed, 23cm/9" cake tin with greaseproof paper.
3. Mix the biscuit crumbs with the melted butter and line the cake tin with it, pressing down firmly. Chill.
4. Place the butter, sugar, cream cheese, flour, orange zest and juice and egg yolks in a large bowl and beat well until smooth.
5. Lightly whip the cream then fold into the mixture. Pour over the crumb base and level the surface.
6. Bake for 1-1½ hours until just set. Turn oven off, open oven door a little and let the cheesecake cool in the oven for another hour. Cool completely on a wire rack.

To make caramelised oranges:

1. Remove all peel and pith from the oranges and slice them thinly, removing any pips. Lay on a dish and sprinkle with 2tbsp of the liqueur.
2. Put the sugar in a heavy saucepan with 150ml/¼ pint water and dissolve sugar over a medium heat.
3. Increase the heat and let the mixture turn a rich caramel colour, remove from heat and carefully add a little more water until you have a thick syrup.
4. Pour over the oranges and allow to cool.
5. Cut the cheesecake into wedges and serve the oranges on the side.

CHOCOLATE ROULADE

(Serves 8-10)

This is the most delicious roulade you will ever eat - it is not cheap to make but if you really want a treat - you have it! Tip - it can be made the day before and also it freezes very well. – *Mary Donohoe*

Ingredients:

350g/12oz Bourneville dark chocolate
5 eggs
175g/6oz castor sugar
150ml/¼ pint double cream
¼ tsp vanilla essence

Method:

1. Preheat oven to 180°C, Gas Mark 4. Line a Swiss roll tin with Bakewell paper.
2. Separate the eggs. Beat the egg yolks and sugar in a bowl until light in colour and thick.
3. Melt the chocolate in the microwave. Remove and add a tablespoon of warm water. Stir vigorously until smooth.
4. Add chocolate to egg yolk mixture.
5. Meanwhile beat the egg whites until stiff in another bowl. Add whites to mixture gently.
6. Pour into tin and bake for 15 minutes. Remove from oven and cover with Bakewell paper and a damp cloth over that.
7. Beat the cream just before serving and add the vanilla essence. Spread over the roulade and holding the Bakewell paper, roll the roulade lengthwise onto a flat serving plate.

TARTE MINUTE

(Serves 6-8)

My mother came over from France during World War II and this is such an easy family recipe that she brought over with her. As the name suggests it really only takes minutes! This tarte freezes well – defrost and heat in oven before serving. - *Jacqueline Young*

Ingredients:

55g/2oz butter or margarine
5 dessertspoons self-raising flour
2 dessertspoons oil
2 eggs
4 dessertspoons sugar
approx 2 cooking apples

Method:

1. Melt butter or margarine and let it cool.
2. Mix together the flour, oil and an egg.
3. Roll out thinly. Line a flan case base with greaseproof paper then line with the pastry.
4. Add sugar and an egg to the melted butter and beat together.
5. Slice apples, neatly to impress or chop roughly if making for the family and place in flan.
6. Pour in cooled mixture.
7. Bake at 200°C, Gas Mark 6 for about 15 minutes.
8. Delicious served warm with ice cream.

FRUITY BREAD AND BUTTER PUDDING

(Serves 6)

This is quite a rich pudding but is perfect comfort food after a long walk on a cold winter's day, although it will put on all the calories you have just taken off. I've often made it when I've been away for a winter weekend because it is easy to transport the ingredients and easy to make. The orange rind/juice makes all the difference. - *Dot Latimer*

Ingredients:

55g/2oz seedless raisins
55g/2oz currants
55g/2oz sultanas
55g/2oz chopped mixed peel
(or if one of the above is not available, then different quantities of the others amounting to the same total weight)
finely grated rind and juice of 1 orange
6 thick slices of bread or toast (I prefer toast)
55g/2oz butter/margarine
110g/4oz soft brown sugar
300ml/½ pint milk
2 eggs
¼ tsp cinnamon

Method:

1. Preheat oven to 190°C, Gas Mark 5.
2. Mix together the dried fruit, orange rind and juice.
3. Butter the toast/bread.
4. Beat the eggs and mix with the milk and cinnamon.
5. Place ½ the fruit mix in the bottom of a buttered baking dish and cover with half the toast/bread and cover with half the sugar.
6. Repeat this process with the other half.
7. Cover these layers with the egg and milk mix.
8. Bake in the oven for about 40 minutes or until crisp on top.
9. Serve with custard, cream or crème fraîche as you wish.

MICROWAVE DUMPLING

(Serves 4)

Here it is Joan! This should have been in the first recipe book as I know it is very popular especially at Christmas time. It came from a Radio Two programme many years ago.

Ingredients:

300ml/½ pint cold water
110g/4oz white sugar
1 tbsp mixed spice
1 tbsp cinnamon
225g/8oz butter
225g/8oz currants
225g/8oz sultanas
1 tbsp treacle
2 eggs, beaten
225g/8oz self raising flour

Method:
1. Put water, sugar, spices, butter, fruit and treacle in a pan.
2. Bring to the boil, simmer for 1 minute.
3. Add to flour, mix in eggs.
4. Put in a bowl lined with cling-film (but DO NOT cover).
5. Cook on HIGH for 9 minutes (850 watt oven). Stand till cool, then empty out.

STICKY TOFFEE PUDDING
(Serves 8)

Fabulous! Everyone enjoys this one. It can be cooked individually in metal pudding basins or in any type of baking dish that allows depth for the pudding to rise, ie pyrex or baking tins. Easily made the day before needed and microwaved to reheat. Can also be frozen.

Ingredients:
175g/6oz stoned dates, roughly chopped
1 tsp bicarbonate of soda
2 tsp Camp coffee essence, optional
75g/2¾oz unsalted butter
175g/6oz caster sugar
3 large eggs
½ tsp pure vanilla extract
225g/8oz self-raising flour, sifted

For the sauce:
225g/8oz dark soft brown sugar
100g/3½oz unsalted butter
300ml/½ pint double cream

Method:
1. Preheat the oven to 180°C, Gas Mark 4.
2. Butter and flour the container you will be using to cook the pudding in, either pudding basins or a large dish.
3. Place the dates in a bowl with the bicarbonate of soda, Camp coffee if using and 300ml/½ pint boiling water. Stir well and set aside.
4. Place the butter and caster sugar in the bowl of an electric mixer and beat well until smooth and fluffy.
5. Beat the eggs with the vanilla extract and pour in a steady stream onto the butter and sugar mixture, beating continuously. Don't be alarmed if the mixture looks curdled at this stage – it will all come together when you add the flour.
6. Add the flour and beat well, then pour in the dates and all the liquid, mix well. Divide the mixture evenly among the pudding basins and place on the middle shelf of the oven.
7. Cook for 20 minutes or until well risen and golden brown. Press the centre of the puddings lightly, if the sponge springs back, they are cooked. Remove from the oven and allow to rest for 5 minutes before turning out onto 8 warmed plates.
8. While the puddings are resting, make the sauce. Place all the ingredients in a pan and heat gently, stir until the sugar has dissolved and the sauce is smooth. Pour a couple of spoonfuls over each pudding and serve the rest in a warm jug.

BAILEYS CRÈME BRÛLÉE

(Serves 6)

This is definitely one for us girls….and easy!

Ingredients:

8 egg yolks

50g/1¾oz caster sugar

450ml/16fl oz double or whipping cream

150ml/5fl oz Baileys Original Irish Cream Liqueur

2 tbsp demerara or caster sugar

Method:

1. Preheat the oven to 150°C, Gas Mark 2.
2. Mix the egg yolks and sugar together in a bowl.
3. Pour the cream and Baileys into a saucepan and bring to the boil.
4. Whisk the flavoured cream into the egg yolks and sugar.
5. Divide the mixture between 6 ramekins. Place them in a deep tray and pour boiling water from the kettle into the tray so it reaches halfway up the ramekins.
6. Cover the tray with foil and bake for 20–35 minutes until just set. To test, there should be a slight wobble in the centre of a ramekin when gently shaken. Remove from the oven and leave to cool. Chill in fridge.
7. Preheat the grill to very hot. Sprinkle the top of the custards with the sugar and place under the grill, watch carefully until the sugar caramelises to a golden brown.

VERY APRICOTTY AND ALMOND ICE CREAM

(Serves 6)

I use tinned apricots but you can use fresh when they are in season. Heavenly.

Ingredients:

750g/1lb10oz apricots, halved and stoned or a 400g tin, drained

2 tbsp lemon juice

2 tbsp runny honey

10 ratafia biscuits (Italian, almond macaroons)

300ml/½ pint whipping cream

Method:

1. Place apricot halves in a saucepan with the lemon juice and honey.
2. Simmer gently until they are meltingly soft, then purée and sieve. Once cool, cover and chill.
3. Put the ratafia biscuits into a small plastic bag and roughly crush them with a rolling pin until you still have fairly large chunks.
4. Whisk the cream in a large bowl until it forms soft peaks, then gently fold in the ratafias and the apricot purée at the same time.
5. Put in a shallow, lidded container and freeze immediately. Leave for 3-4 hours, until firm.
6. To serve, remove from freezer 20 minutes before eating as this helps it soften.

LEMON SYLLABUB

(Serves 6)

A light refreshing syllabub that hardly takes 10 minutes to prepare. Be warned though not to make too far in advance or you will have a puddle of liquid at the bottom of each glass! (A couple of hours is fine).

Ingredients:
400ml/14fl oz whipping cream
200g/7oz lemon curd
½ glass white wine
juice of 1 lemon

To serve:
shortbread or ginger thins
raspberries if possible

Method:
1. Whisk together the lemon curd and cream until it makes soft peaks.
2. Whisk in the wine then the lemon juice to taste.
3. Serve in glasses with 3 raspberries on top and a piece of shortbread or a ginger thin on the side.

BROWN BREAD ICE CREAM

(Serves 6)

This ice cream reminds me of Ireland when I first had it at our dear family friends the Kennedys in Cork. I use Baileys Irish Cream but you can use whisky instead. Lovely served with fudge sauce.

Ingredients:
75g/2¾oz wholemeal breadcrumbs
100g/3½oz caster sugar
300ml/½ pint whipping cream, softly whipped
1 egg
2 tbsp Baileys Original Irish Cream Liqueur

Method:
1. Preheat the oven to 190ºC, Gas Mark 5.
2. Mix the crumbs with the sugar and spread in a layer on a baking tray, lined with tin foil. Bake in the oven until golden and crisp, shaking the tray from time to time. Spread on a cold surface or plate to cool.
3. Separate the egg. Mix the yolk with the liqueur in a cup.
4. Whisk the egg white until stiff, then fold into the whipped cream along with the egg yolk/liqueur mixture. Gently fold in the breadcrumbs.
5. Put in a shallow, lidded container and freeze.

ESPECIALLY CLEVER RASPBERRY SAUCE OR COULIS

I had this last year at Moira's house. This was served poured over peach halves and ice cream, all on one white platter with fresh raspberries and strawberries dotted around the plate and with mint leaves on top. The effect, colours and flavours were fabulous.

Ingredients:
1 jar of good raspberry jam, preferably homemade
a little port or brandy, for that extra zap

Method:
1. Heat jam in a small saucepan until runny then add port or brandy.
2. Sieve and put into a pouring jug.
3. Serve poured over fruit or ice cream.

Bountiful Baking

AUNTY VAL'S CHOCOLATE CAKE

My aunt in Ireland always made my sister Julie's and my birthday cake in the 60's. It was a special request. I was visiting her this year and asked for the story behind it. Whilst she was doing her nursing training in Freemantle, Western Australia and living in the nurses quarters, a friend who lived nearby returned with this yummy cake, which her mother had made. Val has been making it ever since.

Ingredients:
110g/4oz butter
110g/4oz caster sugar
1 egg
175g/6oz self-raising flour
pinch salt
150ml/½ pint milk
50ml/2fl oz boiling water
1½ tbsp cocoa

Method:
1. Preheat oven to 180°C, Gas Mark 4.
2. Cream butter and sugar.
3. Add egg.
4. Mix cocoa with boiling water, add to mixture.
5. Add sifted flour with salt.
6. Finally add milk.
7. Turn into lined 16cm/6¼" ring tin or a deep sided square baking tray. I used a baking tray with deepish sides when I was in Malawi and just iced the top.
8. Bake for about 20 minutes.
9. Ice with chocolate icing of your choice (see page 74 Book Two or page 53 and 54 in Book One).

SOMERSET APPLE CAKE

This recipe was given to me by my church elder Margo Brown. Margo and my church have been very supportive to me over these last 4 years and are great fans of MUMs. This recipe is so easy because the method is rubbing in the margarine or butter so you don't even need a mixer, everything can be prepared in the one bowl and takes about 10 minutes. The mixture is very stiff as there is only a little liquid but this is correct. You can use other fruit – raspberries are delicious.

Ingredients:
225g/8oz self-raising flour
110g/4oz sugar
450g/1lb cooking apples
110g/4oz butter
1 egg

Method:
1. Preheat oven to 180°C, Gas Mark 4.
2. Rub the butter into the flour, add the sugar.
3. Peel, core and chop the apples then add them to the mixture and blend all together with the beaten egg, adding a pinch of ground cloves if desired.
4. Spread mixture in a 20cm/8", well greased shallow tin or a deep flan dish and bake for about 30 minutes.
5. Serve hot, with cream and sprinkled with sugar.

CHEESE AND APPLE SCONES
(Makes 8-10 large scones)

I had the idea to include this recipe and 'arrangement' following a memorable family reunion in Stenying, Brighton. Just think of a warm sunny day, in a typical English village, sitting outside at a little table watching the world go by eating yummy scones and drinking tea. What could be more idyllic?

Ingredients:
450g/1lb self-raising flour
85g/3oz margarine
85g/3oz cheddar cheese, grated (plus a little extra for the tops)
a small apple, skinned and grated (any apple will do)
pinch of salt
pinch of dried English mustard
about 300ml/½ pint milk

Method:
1. Preheat oven to 200°C, Gas Mark 6.
2. Rub margarine into flour until it resembles breadcrumbs.
3. Mix in salt, mustard, grated cheese and apple.
4. Add enough milk to gather all the ingredients together and to roll out.
5. Place on floured surface and gently roll out, still keeping thickness.
6. Using a scone cutter cut out about 8 large scones or more if using a small cutter.
7. Keep gathering up the ends and rolling to make another scone.
8. Wipe the tops of the scones with a little milk and cover with some grated cheese.
9. Bake for 10-15 minutes depending on size.

To serve:
For best effect, take a large white plate and place another smaller white dish in the middle, preferably a higher dish, and place the scones on this. Now take four ramekin style bowls and in one put some red onion marmalade (see Accompaniments chapter). In the others put butter, cream cheese, and lengths of mature cheddar cheese (whatever your favourite is). Now place these dishes around the scones. Make sure everyone has their own side plate, knife and napkin with the teacup on the side. These are quite filling but oh how wonderfully traditional!

JEAN'S MINI CHRISTMAS CAKES - EASY!

I had this in Malawi, the first week we arrived. Jean was a neighbour and friend and invited us for a welcome cup of tea. Jean is a missionary and had been working in Malawi with mothers and children for five years.

Use giant muffin tins.

Ingredients:
1 cup self-raising flour
½ cup brown sugar
½ tsp bicarbonate of soda
1 tsp baking powder
½ cup raisins
½ cup sultanas
4 tbsp mixed peel
100g/3½oz butter
¼ cup cold tea
2 eggs, lightly beaten

Method:
1. Preheat oven to 180°C, Gas Mark 4.
2. In a pan, put raisins, sultanas, mixed peel, butter, tea, and simmer for 4-5 minutes.
3. Cool, then mix in eggs and dry ingredients.
4. Put into greased muffin tins.
5. Bake for about 12-15 minutes.
6. Stand and allow to cool.
7. Put a cherry or some nuts on top.

NUTTY FINGERS

My sister's neighbour John McQueen shared this with us. Tried and tested by Lorna without the walnuts – everyone loved them!

Ingredients:
1 cup self-raising flour
1 cup crushed cornflakes or rice krispies
1 cup desiccated coconut
½ cup sugar
½ cup glacé cherries
½ cup walnuts
110g/4oz margarine, melted

For icing:
175g/6oz icing sugar, sieved
water

Method:
1. Preheat oven to 190°C, Gas Mark 5.
2. Mix dry ingredients together then add margarine and mix well.
3. Press into a swiss roll tin and flatten.
4. Bake for 20 minutes.
5. Ice when warm and leave to cool before cutting into fingers.

IMPRESSIVE GINGERBREAD

My neighbour, Doreen, who is a retired midwife and was a ward sister when I first started my training gave me this recipe that she has shared amongst her friends and with me. It is amazing, easy and gorgeous. Well worth buying loaf liners from Lakeland.

Ingredients:
110g/4oz margarine
175ml/6fl oz water
175g/6oz caster sugar
1 tbsp syrup
1 tbsp treacle
175g/6oz raisins
175g/6oz sultanas

Lightly simmer the above in a large pan for 10 minutes.

Add:
350g/12oz plain flour
½ tsp salt
1 tsp mixed spice
1 tsp ginger
1 tsp bicarbonate of soda
1 egg, beaten

Mix well.
Put into a 900g/2lb loaf tin.
Bake at 180°C, Gas Mark 4 for approx 1 hour.

RASPBERRY OATMEAL BARS

(Makes 24 bars)
An old favourite rather like flapjacks but the raspberries make it a little bit different.

Ingredients:
¾ cup unsalted butter, softened
1 cup brown sugar
1½ cups plain flour
1½ cups rolled oats
1 tsp salt
½ tsp bicarbonate of soda
1 jar raspberry jam

Method:
1. Preheat oven to 200°C, Gas Mark 6.
2. Cream butter and sugar until light and fluffy.
3. Combine flour, oats, salt and bicarbonate and mix thoroughly with butter/sugar mixture.
4. Press half the crumb mixture into a greased 20cm/8" square baking tin. Spread with jam and sprinkle the remaining crumb mixture over top.
5. Bake for 20-25 minutes.
6. When cold, cut into bars.

TRIPLE CHOCOLATE BROWNIES

Credit goes to Sainsburys for this recipe and I usually use Sainsbury's Luxury Belgian Chocolate and their unrefined golden caster sugar. I suggest using a lower temperature for an extra 10 minutes and leave in tin overnight to cool for a firmer cut and I find they hold their shape better. – *Laura Thomson & Rona Ferguson*

Ingredients:
200g/7oz plain chocolate
50g/1¾oz milk chocolate
200g/7oz white chocolate
225g/8oz butter
4 medium eggs
325g/11½oz unrefined golden caster sugar
2 x 5ml tsp vanilla essence
150g/5½oz plain flour
pinch salt

Method:
1. Preheat oven to 180°C, Gas Mark 4.
2. Line a cake tin, 28cm x 18cm x 6cm/ 11"x 7"x 2 ½", with parchment/baking paper.
3. Melt milk and plain chocolate with the butter and allow to cool slightly.
4. Beat the eggs, sugar and vanilla essence together.
5. Roughly chop the white chocolate into small pieces.
6. Whisk the chocolate mixture into the egg mixture then fold in the flour, salt and white chocolate.
7. Pour into the tin, and bake for approximately 35-40 minutes or until the top is pale and crisp and the centre is almost set. Put an ovenproof dish with some water in it into the oven at the same time to keep the humidity up in the oven and this will stop the brownies drying out.
8. Cool on a wire tray in the tin (preferably overnight) then cut into 20 pieces.

SANDY'S CHOCOLATE BISCUITS

Had this in Malawi on a business trip for MUMs in May 2008. Sandy is from South Africa and this recipe was given to her by her friend Zita from the Seychelles. I sat in Sandy's garden and ate at least six of these biscuits, they really hit the spot!

Ingredients:
225g/8oz margarine
125g/4½oz sugar
200g/7oz plain flour, sifted
100g/3½oz coconut
1 tbsp cocoa
100g/3½oz rolled oats
½ tsp baking powder

For the icing:
icing sugar
1 tbsp cocoa
warm water

Method:
1. Mix everything together.
2. Roll into balls, place on baking tray and flatten with a fork.
3. Bake at 180ºC, Gas Mark 4 for approx 30 minutes.
4. Ice when cold.

NEVER FAIL PASTRY

I was useless at pastry but this "no touch - keep cold" version works every time and I always freeze it and then defrost it. Hope it works for you. It came from a late friend, Dennis who lived in Spain and generously shared his recipe.
The secret is to keep everything cold and don't mix by hand, but in a mixer. Make in advance and freeze in batches and then defrost in the fridge. *– Chris Boyden and Barrie Manley*

Ingredients:

For mince pies:
175g/6oz plain flour
110g/4oz butter
40g/1½oz caster sugar
2 egg yolks
splash of cold water

For tarts:
225g/8oz plain flour
135g/5oz margarine or butter
55g/2oz sugar
1 cold egg
salt

For quiches:
350g/12oz plain flour
175g/6oz butter
pinch salt
1 cold egg
splash of cold water
juice of ½ cold lemon

Method:
You can check the method with your mixer instructions but I usually do the following.
1. Sieve the flour into the mixer.
2. Cut up the butter or margarine and add. Mix on short one second bursts to make breadcrumbs.
3. Add the dry ingredients and mix.
4. Finally add the egg and liquids.
5. Mix until the dough has come together in a ball.
6. It is now ready to use or freeze.

MILLIONAIRE SHORTBREAD

This is my favourite recipe for Millionaire Shortbread. My mum was a fantastic baker and always had a supply of these in the cupboard. Perfect for Scots with a sweet tooth and delicious with a cup of tea!! - *Stephen Jardine*

Ingredients:
Base:
175g/6oz plain flour
75g/2¾oz cornflour
75g/2¾oz golden caster sugar
175g/6oz salted butter, slightly softened

Topping:
2 x 400g tins condensed milk
300g/10½oz good chocolate (half milk, half plain)

Method:
1. Preheat oven to 180°C, Gas Mark 4.
2. Sift the flour and cornflour into a bowl and then mix in the sugar and butter and work into a firm ball.
3. Press the shortbread mix into a lightly greased swiss roll tin 33cm x 23cm/13" x 9". Prick with a fork and bake for 25 minutes. Cool in the tin.
4. To make the caramel, place tins unopened in a heavy saucepan, cover with water and simmer for 2 hours. Keep topped up and make sure they don't boil dry.
5. Afterwards allow the cans to cool.
6. Spread caramel over the base then melt the chocolate and spread over the top.
7. Allow it to set then cut into squares and enjoy.

TOFFEE TIFFIN

I am one of the baking co-ordinators at our Church and am always on the lookout for good easy recipes. Basically this is very similar to the Tiffin in Book 1 but it is an alternative version which has proved very popular. Also good using shortbread for a third of the biscuits. – *Anne Scullion*

Ingredients:
200g/7oz dark chocolate

For the filling:
397g tin condensed milk
25 digestive biscuits, crushed
4 tbsp cocoa powder
4 tbsp coconut
4 tbsp drinking chocolate
110g/4oz margarine

Method:
1. Boil the unopened tin of condensed milk for 45 minutes in a pan making sure it is always fully covered with boiling water.
2. Line a tray, 20cm x 30cm, 8" x 12" with greaseproof paper.
3. Melt 100g/3½oz chocolate and spread over the greaseproof paper and leave to set.
4. Melt the margarine and mix all the filling ingredients together. Spread over top of the chocolate.
5. Melt the remaining 100g/3½oz chocolate and spread over the top. Put in the fridge to set and cut when firm.

LEMONY FUDGE SLICE
This makes a change from chocolate tray bakes and is very quick and yummy.

Ingredients:
450g/1lb rich tea biscuits
100g/3½oz desiccated coconut
grated rind of 1 lemon
200g/7oz butter
397g tin condensed milk

Icing:
175g /6oz icing sugar, sieved
lemon juice

Method:
1. Crush the biscuits then add the coconut and lemon rind.
2. Melt the butter and add the condensed milk.
3. Add to the dry ingredients and mix.
4. Press into a greased traybake tin.
5. Mix the icing sugar with sufficient lemon juice to be able to spread over the tray and leave to set. Cut into squares.

FUDGE SLICE
It's just like eating fudge, but easier to make. Thanks Doreen!

Ingredients:
225g/8oz digestive biscuits, finely crushed
225g/8oz butter
225g/8oz sugar
397g tin condensed milk
200g/7oz chocolate (plain, milk or white)

Method:
1. Melt butter, sugar and condensed milk together over a low heat until the sugar has dissolved.
2. Bring to the boil and boil for 3-5 minutes stirring continuously. Mixture will have thickened.
3. Remove from heat and add biscuit crumbs.
4. Pour into a traybake tin and leave to set.
5. Melt the chocolate and spread over the top.
6. Cut into small squares when cold.

"Kauma feeding station was set up by MUMs in April 2009. Over 100 orphaned and malnourished children in this area are now benefiting from three nutritious meals a week made by volunteers. The 'Joyful Motherhood' programme based in Bwaila hospital has been delighted to welcome the help and support from the people of Scotland through the MUMs charity."

Beatrice Namale
Community Nurtitional Specialist for 'Joyful Motherhood'

CRAIGIE'S KITCHEN

Craigie's Farm Deli and Café.

John and Kirsteen Sinclair run a very successful family business at their farm just outside Edinburgh near the Forth Road Bridge. The farm won the Glenfiddich Food Award in 2008 due to the quality of their excellent food and service and it is no surprise that their popularity has grown and they are now extending the shop and café. This has all happened in the last year. My family and friends are frequent visitors and we all love the food! Everything is seasonal, home grown and made on the premises, even the jams and chutneys. Craigie's have a unique community spirit and have been a great support to MUMs Recipes through selling the recipe books in the shop.

I am delighted they are happy to share a sample of the many wonderful dishes which are served in the café.

We have served all of these at some point on the Craigie's menu and the ingredients are available in the shop so I hope you enjoy these recipes and should you have any difficulty come in and ask any member of the Craigie's team. - *Anne Baird, Catering Manager*

LEEK AND POTATO SOUP
(Serves 4)

Ingredients:
3 onions
3 potatoes
3 leeks
Swiss Marigold gluten free stock

Method:
Peel and roughly chop onions and potatoes, put into pan.
Cut nearly all of the green apart from 3cm/1¼" from the leeks, discard green, roughly chop and add to pan. Add enough water to cover vegetables in pan keeping a note so as to add correct amount of stock. We use Swiss Marigold Gluten Free; measure out stock as per instructions.
Boil first then turn heat down to a gentle simmer and cook until potatoes are tender. Whiz with blender and season if required. Add a little cream, just perfect.

SWEET POTATO AND RED PEPPER SOUP
(Serves 4)

Ingredients:
3 sweet potatoes, peeled and chopped
1 onion, peeled and chopped
2 red peppers, roasted in oven to get skins off
Swiss Marigold stock

Method:
This is a very quick and tasty soup; peppers are tastier when roasted first in the oven. Put all prepared vegetables in a pan and cover with enough water to start to boil, keep note of the amount and then mix in stock as per the instructions. To make it posh, when serving add a little blob of cream or crème fraîche and swirl that with a skewer.

PORK CASSEROLE
(Serves 4)

Ingredients:
450g/1lb stewing Pork, British, cubed
1 tbsp plain flour
1 tin chopped tomatoes
1 tbsp brown sugar
2 tbsp vinegar
1 tbsp Worcester sauce
1 tsp garlic powder or 2 cloves, crushed
1 tsp ground ginger
110g/4ozs mushrooms

Method:
Put meat and flour and salt and pepper into plastic bag and shake, put in pan and fry gently until pork is golden in colour. Keep warm in casserole dish.
To pan add tomatoes, sugar, vinegar, Worcester sauce, garlic, ginger and mushrooms. Heat through to simmering and then pour over meat and cook for 1½ hrs at 180°C, Gas Mark 4. Serve with a light salad and or a jacket potato.
A great tasty supper dish. Support your local pig farmer there are very few left so buy British, please.

COUSCOUS SALAD
(Serves 4)

Ingredients:
250g/9oz couscous combined with equal volume of boiling water (vegetable stock)
20ml olive oil
1 clove garlic, peeled and crushed
½ mild chilli pepper, deseeded and sliced finely
1 red pepper, deseeded and cut into 1.5cm strips
1 red onion, peeled and coarsely chopped
150g/5½oz mushrooms, quartered
15 black olives, halved
1 tbsp chopped coriander and parsley
freshly milled black pepper
pinch of salt
juice of ½ lemon or orange

Dressing:
1 tsp honey
1 tsp wholegrain mustard
2 tsp Craigie's Raspberry Vinegar

Method:
Preheat the oven to 190°C, Gas Mark 5. Toss garlic, chilli, pepper, onion and mushrooms in the scant oil and open roast on a baking tray for about 20 minutes. Give the tray a gentle shake halfway through cooking time to evenly cook. Meanwhile place couscous in a generously sized bowl and add equivalent volume of boiling water. Fluff up with a fork and set aside for the liquid to absorb. Once the couscous is ready, combine all the ingredients and serve warm or cold.

RASPBERRY CRUNCH
(Serves 4)

Ingredients:
1 pkt ginger nuts, bashed in a poly bag
an equal quantity of frozen raspberries or more if you like, bashed in a poly bag
whipped cream

Method:
This is fun to do and an easy one if you have little helpers in the kitchen. The trick to this is keeping the raspberries frozen.
First bash biscuits, then whip cream, finally bash rasps. In a see through bowl, if you have one, put raspberries in first, cover with biscuits, then cream. If you have plenty put another layer on top. Yummy!

VICTORIA SPONGE

Ingredients:
225g/8oz butter
225g/8oz caster sugar
4 large eggs at room temperature
225g/8oz self-raising flour, sifted
1 tsp baking powder
1 tsp vanilla essence
2 x 23cm/24cm, 9"/9 ½" baking tins, greased, with easily removable bottoms if possible

Method:
We basically melt the butter then add all other ingredients and mix to a light and fluffy texture, no more than 5 minutes (too much air makes cakes bubbly on top). Split equally into already greased tins.
Bake in oven at 180°C, Gas Mark 4 for approx 25-30 minutes or when cake starts to leave side of tin. Leave to cool for 5 minutes in tin, then take out and cool on wire rack.

For Filling:
raspberry jam, homemade or Craigie's
butter icing – 110g/4oz butter and 225g/8oz icing sugar, mix well together add a little vanilla essence if you like.
Cover top of one of the sponges with raspberry jam and butter icing. Put other sponge on top and cover with butter icing. Decorate as fancy or as plain as you like.

Through the Rose Project, friends of MUMs have helped build this magnificent Wellness Centre for Nurses, Midwives and other health care workers to provide counselling on HIV and AIDS, other ailments, and psychosocial and spiritual care and support plus base for home based care. Without your support, half of the building or works you are seeing here would not have been nor the services envisaged.

Your extension of the same support to Nurse/Midwife Charity cannot go unnoticed and appreciated. You are helping to serve many women and babies in the Lilongwe area who are being taken care of by Nurse Charity at her clinic.

We greatly appreciate your continued support.

BRAVO MUMS !

God bless you all

Dorothy Ngoma
EXECUTIVE DIRECTOR
Nurses & Midwives Association of Malawi

ACCOMPANIMENTS

PARSNIP BAKE

(Serves 4)

This recipe came from Lorna's mother-in-law and it goes down a treat with Sunday dinner.

Ingredients:
675g/1½lbs parsnips (after peeling)
225g/8oz onions, chopped
85g/3oz margarine
3 eggs, beaten
3 tbsp single cream
salt and pepper

Method:
1. Cook parsnips until soft.
2. Fry onions in margarine until soft and lightly browned.
3. Purée together the parsnips, onion, eggs and cream.
4. Season well.
5. Pour into a buttered dish and bake in oven at 200°C, Gas Mark 6 until golden and set.

MUJEDERA

This is the Middle Eastern equivalent of Fish and Chips. It is a combination that is much greater than its single parts and costs pennies. – *Alec and Elisabeth Harden*

Ingredients:
1 cup rice
1 cup brown lentils
2 onions, sliced
garlic
cumin

To serve:
natural yoghurt
cucumber
tomatoes

Method:
1. Wash rice and soak in salted water.
2. Boil lentils until tender. Add rice and water to cover plus 2.5cm/1". Add salt, pepper, cumin. Bring to boil and simmer until rice is tender.
3. Meanwhile fry the sliced onions and garlic in olive oil, mix some into lentil rice mix. Fry the rest until crisp.
4. Serve with crisp onions on top and yoghurt, finely chopped cucumber and tomato alongside.

LIZZIE'S SALSA

Specially loved and put together by Lizzie Arnot, aged 13.

Ingredients:
4 large ripe tomatoes
bunch of spring onions
fresh coriander
1 lime
olive oil

Method:
1. Take the skins off the tomatoes by immersing in boiling water for about a minute.
2. De-seed and clean out the middles of the tomatoes, then chop into fairly small bits.
3. Finely chop 4 or 5 spring onions.
4. Finely chop a good sized bunch of coriander leaves.
5. Add all the ingredients together and mix well with the juice of the lime and drizzle in a little olive oil and mix well again.
6. Serve as a side dish or mix with rice (Lizzie's favourite) or spread on garlic bread.

BRONAGH'S SALSA
(Serves 6 people as a side salad)
The amount of ingredients will depend on how many you are serving. Easily adjusted to produce a bowl of salsa salad. - *Bronagh Finlay*

Ingredients:
3-4 large tomatoes, chopped
1 red onion, finely chopped
2 garlic cloves, crushed
1 red pepper, finely chopped
1 red chilli, seeds removed, finely chopped
fresh basil or coriander
1 avocado, chopped
olive oil
juice of ½ lemon
juice of ½ lime

Method:
1. Simply chop everything small and mix well together.
2. Drizzle over some olive oil with lemon and lime juices finishing with a good grinding of black pepper.
3. Preferably serve in a white bowl as the contrasting colours look wonderful.

MANGO SALSA
(Serves 4)
Great with salmon or trout or just for dipping.

Ingredients:
1 mango, peeled and diced
½ small red onion, chopped finely
½ each small red and green pepper, chopped
1cm/½" piece root ginger, peeled and chopped finely
1cm/½" piece cucumber, chopped
1 small chilli, chopped finely
juice of ½ small lemon
juice of ½ small lime
60ml/2fl oz fresh orange juice
2 tbsp coriander, chopped

Method:
1. Mix everything together.
2. Put in jam jar and leave in fridge to develop flavours.

ALI'S SPICED APRICOT AND ORANGE CHUTNEY

(Makes 1 litre)

The delicious, spiced apricot chutney recipe was shared at an Advent Afternoon at church, where people came along with their favourite seasonal ideas for gifts and decorations and gave others a chance both to make and to taste new things.

It was great to be able to add other people's Christmas traditions in to the mix of our own Advent preparations. The chutney's fresh, spicy flavours mature in around 3-4 weeks and it makes a lovely gift with the top tied in fabric or a circle of Christmas paper. - *Ali Brown*

Ingredients:

400g/14oz no soak apricots
1 tsp whole coriander seeds
225g/8oz soft light brown sugar
425ml/15fl oz cider vinegar
1 medium onion, chopped
50g/1¾oz sultanas
3 tbsp root ginger, finely grated
2 garlic cloves, finely chopped
1 level tbsp salt
½ tsp cayenne pepper
grated zest and juice of 1 small orange

Method:

1. Chop apricots into smallish chunks and place in a large pan.
2. Place coriander seeds in small pan and heat pan while tossing seeds around – as soon as they begin to splutter transfer to pestle and mortar and crush lightly before sprinkling over apricots.
3. Add remaining ingredients to the apricots and heat gently stirring until the sugar crystals have dissolved.
4. Bring everything to simmering point and let chutney simmer (covered) for 45 minutes – 1 hour. The apricots and onions need to be quite tender. The right consistency is like chunky jam rather than liquid jam. It will thicken as it cools down.
5. When ready, spoon into warm sterilised jars and seal straight away.
6. Label when cool.
7. Best kept for 1 month before eating.

APPLE AND PEAR CHUTNEY

(Makes 4 jam jars)

This is a great way to use up the garden fruit, and can be used straightaway without maturing. Lovely with cheese and cold ham.

Ingredients:

6 pears, cored and chopped into small pieces (leave the peel on for extra flavour and nutrients)
2 large Bramley apples, cored and chopped into small pieces (with the peel left on)
1 large red onion, finely chopped
12 cherry tomatoes, quartered
400g/14oz brown sugar

150g/5½oz sultanas
75g/2¾oz dried figs, chopped
500ml/18fl oz cider vinegar
250ml/9fl oz still cider
1 tbsp Dijon mustard
3 garlic cloves, finely chopped
½ tsp ground cinnamon
½ tsp ground ginger

Method:
1. Put all ingredients into a large stainless steel saucepan. Heat up and cook over a very low heat, stirring often, until all the sugar has dissolved. Simmer gently for about 1–1½ hours. The mixture will be thick and rich.
2. Spoon into warm sterilised jars, seal and store in a cool dark place. Chutney should keep for 6 months unopened but after opening keep it in the fridge and eat quickly.

GREEN TOMATO CHUTNEY

This is an old recipe from my Aunt Cherry. Her footnote to the original recipe was; "This is very delicious." Everyone in our family agrees! – *Esmé Chapman*

Ingredients:
2.7kg/6lb green tomatoes
900g/2lb apples
1.4kg/3lb Demerara sugar
1.4kg/3lb onions
¼ lb salt
1.2 litres/1 quart vinegar (white malt)
1½ tsp white pepper
1 tsp ground mace
1 tsp cayenne pepper
110g/4oz mustard seed (light colour)
1 bay leaf
6 bruised cloves

Method:
1. Chop tomatoes.
2. Core apples and chop.
3. Peel and slice onions.
4. Cook all these in vinegar for 1 hour.
5. Add sugar, cloves, mace, pepper, mustard seed, salt, cayenne pepper and bayleaf and cook again for 1½ hours – till a spoon leaves a trail on the surface.
6. Bottle and seal immediately.

RED ONION MARMALADE

Can be made several days ahead to allow the flavours to develop. Delicious with steaks, lamb, chicken or omelettes. - *Diana Miller*

Ingredients:
6 red onions, thinly sliced
⅓ cup balsamic vinegar
1 tbsp honey
¼ tsp sea salt
freshly ground pepper

Method:
1. Place the onions in a heavy-based saucepan and add the vinegar, honey, salt and pepper.
2. Bring to a simmer over medium heat and continue to simmer for about 15 minutes, stirring frequently, until the liquid has evaporated.
3. Remove the pan from the heat and let cool.
4. Transfer to an airtight container and store in the fridge.

JALAPENO JELLY

Handling chilli peppers comes with a warning! They can burn your skin so wear gloves if you have sensitive skin.
The "heat" of the jelly depends on how many seeds you leave in the jalapenos. I usually leave the seeds in one pepper. This jelly is great with cheese or with chicken, fish or meat. It's also great in the Quesadillas earlier in the book. – *Diana Miller*

Ingredients:
3 fresh green jalapenos (chillies)
1 green pepper
675g/1lb 8oz sugar
125ml/4fl oz cider vinegar
75ml/2½fl oz Certo (pectin)
2 tbsp fresh lime juice

Method:
1. Process jalapenos and green pepper in a food processor until smooth.
2. Combine pepper purée, sugar and vinegar in a heavy pan.
3. Bring to a boil over a medium-high heat, stirring constantly. Boil for 3 minutes.
4. Stir in Certo (pectin) and lime juice. Boil, stirring constantly, for 1 minute.
5. Remove from the heat and skim off foam with a metal spoon.
6. Pour into warm sterilized jars and seal.

BREADCRUMBS

A great way to use up heels, crusts and left over bread. Keep in the freezer and there is no need to defrost before use. Can be used on top of casseroles mixed with grated cheese. Handy for adding to hamburger mix.

Method for fresh breadcrumbs:
1. Using a food processor, whiz any bread until it resembles crumbs.

Method for dried breadcrumbs:
1. Follow instructions for fresh breadcrumbs.
2. Preheat oven to 180°C, Gas Mark 4.
3. Lay crumbs on a baking tray and put in the oven.
4. Turn the oven off and leave the crumbs in the oven to dry in the oven to dry out overnight.

Drawing by Lara Meguid

THE STRANGER

I help the midwife make the bed, a sheet
Of plastic first, to keep the mattress clean,
And then the draw-sheet, folded twice. I void
The thoughts of beds they dig by spade and fix
My mind on how to count the gaps between
The pains and when to push but still do not
Expect this gale force ten and you. Your head's
A bulb that's breaking through the self of me.

I see you crooked within your father's arm
As in a nest. One day I'll love you more
Than I can guess. Right now, resentful, tired,
Undone, I love and hate you all in one,
Reclaim myself and watch you from afar
And wonder – wonder who on earth you are.

'The Stranger' was written about the birth of my daughter, Kate.
It was a rather difficult home birth and I was very frightened. - *Diana Hendry*

From: Making Blue (Peterloo Poets) by **Diana Hendry**

INDEX